Śrī Prabandhāvalī

śrī śrī guru-gaurāṅgau jayataḥ

ŚRĪ PRABANDHĀVALĪ

A Collection of Devotional Essays

Śrī Śrīmad Bhaktivedānta Nārāyaṇa Mahārāja

Vṛndāvana, Uttar Pradesh, India

Other titles by Śrīla Nārāyaṇa Mahārāja:

The Nectar of Govinda-līlā
Going Beyond Vaikuṇṭha
Bhakti-rasāyana
Śrī Śikṣāṣṭaka
Veṇu-gīta
Śrī Bhakti-rasāmṛta-sindhu-bindu
Śrī Manaḥ-śikṣā
Bhakti-tattva-viveka
Pinnacle of Devotion
Śrī Upadeśāmṛta
Arcana-dīpikā
The Essence of All Advice
Śrī Gauḍīya Gīti-guccha
Dāmodara-līlā-mādhurī
Śrīmad Bhagavad-gītā
Śrīmad Bhakti Prajñāna Keśava Gosvāmī – His Life and Teachings
Five Essential Essays
Śrī Harināma Mahā-mantra
Secret Truths of the Bhāgavata
Jaiva-dharma
Beyond Nirvāṇa
Śrī Vraja-maṇḍala Parikramā
Śrī Bhajana-rahasya
Śrī Brahma-saṁhitā
The Origin of Ratha-yātrā
Rays of the Harmonist (periodical)

For further information, visit www.purebhakti.com

ISBN 81-86737-00-6

First printing: April 1996 – 2,000 copies
Second printing: October 2003 – 5,000 copies

CONTENTS

INTRODUCTION

It is a matter of great happiness that we can now present this second edition of *Śrī Prabandhāvalī* before our Vaiṣṇava readers. This book is a compilation of lectures spoken originally in Hindi by our most worshipful Śrīla Gurudeva, *oṁ viṣṇupāda aṣṭottara-śata* Śrī Śrīmad Bhaktivedānta Nārāyaṇa Mahārāja. The first edition of this book was published in 1996, just before Śrīla Gurudeva's first preaching tour of Western countries.

Observing the festival days outlined in the Vaiṣṇava calendar is an important aspect of devotional practice. Śrīla Gurudeva always speaks on the appropriate topic on such days, whether it be the appearance or disappearance day of a prominent Vaiṣṇava *ācārya*, the appearance day of an incarnation of Bhagavān, or any other significant day. Of the eleven lectures included within this book, nine are lectures that he spoke on significant dates from the Vaiṣṇava calendar. The word *prabandha* means an essay and *āvalī* means a collection. We are confident that devotees will find this *Śrī Prabandhāvalī* helpful in their sincere efforts to honour these important days.

The material herein was spoken during 1989 and 1991 at Śrī Keśavajī Gauḍīya Maṭha in Mathurā and Śrī Rūpa-Sanātana Gauḍīya Maṭha in Vṛndāvana. The only exception is the chapter on Śrīla A.C. Bhaktivedānta Swami Prabhupāda, which was compiled from three separate lectures spoken in English in the early 1990s.

In this second edition a glossary has been added to assist readers unfamiliar with Sanskrit terminology. Also, the book has been redesigned and typeset to a higher standard. Acknowledgment goes to Lavaṅga-latā dāsī for copy-editing this second edition, to Ṛṣabhādeva dāsa and Śānti dāsī for proofreading the final manuscript, to Atula-kṛṣṇa dāsa for checking the Sanskrit, to Kṛṣṇa-prema dāsa for designing the new cover and to Subala-sakhā dāsa for providing the new photograph of Śrīla Gurudeva. This publication is yet another manifestation of Śrīla Gurudeva's great mercy. Together we offer it into his hands and pray that he will bless us with the necessary qualification to continue serving him in this way. Hare Kṛṣṇa.

An aspiring servant of the Vaiṣṇavas,

Prema-vilāsa dāsa

Guru-pūrṇimā
13th July, 2003
Gopīnātha-bhavana, Śrī Vṛndāvana

MAṄGALĀCARAṆA

vande 'haṁ śrī-guroḥ śrī-yuta-pada-kamalaṁ
śrī-gurūn vaiṣṇavāṁś ca
śrī-rūpaṁ sāgrajātaṁ saha-gaṇa-raghunāthān-
vitaṁ taṁ sa-jīvam
sādvaitaṁ sāvadhūtaṁ parijana-sahitaṁ
kṛṣṇa-caitanya-devaṁ
śrī-rādhā-kṛṣṇa-pādān saha-gaṇa-lalitā-
śrī-viśākhānvitaṁś ca

I offer *praṇāma* unto the lotus feet of *śrī gurudeva* – which includes the *dīkṣā-guru*, the *bhajana-śikṣā-guru*, the superlative succession of *gurus* predominated by Śrī Madhvācārya and Śrī Mādhavendra Purī, and the Vaiṣṇavas of all four *yugas* – to Śrī Rūpa Gosvāmī, his elder brother Śrī Sanātana Gosvāmī, Raghunātha dāsa Gosvāmī, Jīva Gosvāmī and their associates, to Śrī Advaita Ācārya, Śrī Nityānanda Prabhu, Śrī Caitanya Mahāprabhu and all of His associates, and to Śrī Rādhā-Kṛṣṇa accompanied by all of Their *sakhīs* and *mañjarīs* headed by Śrī Lalitā and Viśākhā.

Śrī Guru-praṇāma

oṁ ajñāna-timirāndhasya
jñānāñjana-śalākayā
cakṣur unmīlitaṁ yena
tasmai śrī-gurave namaḥ

I offer my most humble *daṇḍavat-praṇāma* unto *śrī guru*, who with the torchlight of knowledge has opened my eyes, which were blinded by the darkness of ignorance.

nama oṁ viṣṇu-pādāya
ācārya-siṁha-rūpiṇe
śrī śrīmad bhakti-prajñāna-
keśava iti nāmine

atimartya-caritrāya
svāśritānāṁ ca pāline
jīva-duḥkhe sadārttāya
śrī-nāma-prema-dāyine

I offer *praṇāma* unto my most worshipful *śrī gurudeva*, the lion-like *ācārya jagad-guru oṁ viṣṇupāda aṣṭottara-śata* Śrī Śrīmad Bhakti Prajñāna Keśava Gosvāmī, who is a thoroughly transcendental personality, who nurtures with great affection those who have taken shelter of him, who is always sad to see the sufferings of souls inimical to Kṛṣṇa, and who bestows love for the holy name.

Śrīla Prabhupāda-vandanā

nama oṁ viṣṇu-pādāya
kṛṣṇa-preṣṭhāya bhūtale
śrīmate bhaktisiddhānta-
sarasvatīti nāmine

śrī-vārṣabhānavī-devī-
dayitāya kṛpābdhaye
kṛṣṇa-sambandha-vijñāna-
dāyine prabhave namaḥ

I offer *praṇāma* time and again unto the master who bestows the science of Kṛṣṇa, who is very dear to Kṛṣṇa, who is the recipient of Śrī Vārṣabhānavī-devī Rādhikā's mercy, who is an ocean of mercy and who appeared on this earth as *oṁ viṣṇupāda* Śrīmad Bhaktisiddhānta Sarasvatī Gosvāmī.

mādhuryojjvala-premāḍhya-
śrī-rūpānuga-bhaktida
śrī-gaura-karuṇā-śakti-
vigrahāya namo 'stu te

I offer *praṇāma* unto he who is the embodiment of that *rūpānuga-bhakti* which is radiant with the amorous love of Śrī Rādhā and Kṛṣṇa and who is the personification of Śrī Gaurāṅga Mahāprabhu's mercy potency.

namas te gaura-vāṇī
śrī-mūrtaye dīna-tāriṇe
rūpānuga-viruddhāpa-
siddhānta-dhvānta-hāriṇe

I offer *praṇāma* unto he who is the embodiment of Mahāprabhu's teachings, who is the deliverer of the fallen and who is the annihilator of the darkness arising from misconceptions opposed to the philosophy enunciated by Śrīla Rūpa Gosvāmī.

Śrīla Gaura-kiśora-vandanā

namo gaura-kiśorāya
sākṣād-vairāgya-mūrtaye
vipralambha-rasāmbhodhe
pādāmbujāya te namaḥ

I offer *praṇāma* unto the lotus feet of Śrīla Gaura-kiśora dāsa Bābājī Mahārāja, who is renunciation personified and an ocean of *vipralambha-rasa.*

Śrīla Bhaktivinoda-vandanā

namo bhaktivinodāya
saccidānanda-nāmine
gaura-śakti-svarūpāya
rūpānuga-varāya te

I offer *praṇāma* unto Saccidānanda Śrī Bhaktivinoda, who is the foremost of *rūpānuga* devotees and the embodiment of Śrī Caitanya Mahāprabhu's *śakti.*

Śrīla Jagannātha-vandanā

gaurāvirbhāva-bhūmes tvaṁ
nirdeṣṭā sajjana-priyaḥ
vaiṣṇava-sārvabhauma-śrī-
jagannāthāya te namaḥ

I offer *praṇāma* unto Vaiṣṇava-sārvabhauma Śrī Jagannātha dāsa Bābājī Mahārāja, who verified the precise location of Śrī Gaurasundara's appearance and who is dear to all saintly persons.

Śrī Vaiṣṇava-vandanā

vāñchā-kalpatarubhyaś ca
kṛpā-sindhubhya eva ca
patitānāṁ pāvanebhyo
vaiṣṇavebhyo namo namaḥ

I offer *praṇāma* unto the Vaiṣṇavas, who just like desire trees can fulfil the desires of everyone and who are full of compassion for conditioned souls.

Śrīman Mahāprabhu-vandanā

namo mahā-vadānyāya
kṛṣṇa-prema-pradāya te
kṛṣṇāya kṛṣṇa-caitanya-
nāmne gaura-tviṣe namaḥ

I offer *praṇāma* unto Śrī Caitanya Mahāprabhu, who is Kṛṣṇa Himself. He has assumed the golden hue of Śrīmatī Rādhikā and is munificently distributing *kṛṣṇa-prema*.

Śrī Kṛṣṇa-praṇāma

he kṛṣṇa karuṇā-sindho
dīna-bandho jagat-pate
gopeśa gopikā-kānta
rādhā-kānta namo 'stu te

I offer *praṇāma* unto Śrī Kṛṣṇa, who is an ocean of mercy, the friend of the distressed and the source of creation. He is the master of the *gopas* and the lover of the *gopīs* headed by Śrīmatī Rādhikā.

Śrī Rādhā-praṇāma

tapta-kāñcana-gaurāṅgi
rādhe vṛndāvaneśvari
vṛṣabhānu-sute devi
praṇamāmi hari-priye

I offer *praṇāma* unto Śrīmatī Rādhikā, whose complexion is like molten gold and who is the queen of Vṛndāvana. She is the daughter of Vṛṣabhānu Mahārāja and is very dear to Śrī Kṛṣṇa.

Śrī Sambandhādhideva-praṇāma

jayatāṁ suratau paṅgor
mama manda-mater gatī
mat-sarvasva-padāmbhojau
rādhā-madana-mohanau

All glories to the supremely merciful Śrī Rādhā-Madana-mohana! Although I am lame and foolish, They are my refuge, and Their lotus feet are my everything.

Śrī Abhidheyādhideva-praṇāma

dīvyad-vṛndāraṇya-kalpa-drumādhaḥ
śrīmad-ratnāgāra-siṁhāsana-sthau
śrīmad-rādhā-śrīla-govinda-devau
preṣṭhālībhiḥ sevyamānau smarāmi

I meditate upon Śrīmatī Rādhikā and Śrīmān Govindadeva, who are seated on an effulgent *siṁhāsana* beneath a desire tree in a temple composed of jewels in the supremely beautiful land of Śrī Vṛndāvana, accepting service from Their beloved *sakhīs* headed by Lalitā and Viśākhā.

Śrī Prayojanādhideva-praṇāma

śrīmān rāsa-rasārambhī
vaṁśī-vaṭa-taṭa-sthitaḥ
karṣan veṇu-svanair gopīr
gopīnāthaḥ śriye 'stu naḥ

May that Śrī Gopīnātha, who originated the transcendental mellow of the *rāsa-līlā* and who stands at Vaṁśīvaṭa attracting the *gopīs* with the melody of His flute, bestow His benediction upon me.

Śrī Tulasī-praṇāma

vṛndāyai tulasī-devyai
priyāyai keśavasya ca
kṛṣṇa-bhakti-prade devi
satyavatyai namo namaḥ

I offer *praṇāma* time and again to Tulasī-devī, who, also known as Vṛndā and Satyavatī, is very dear to Śrī Kṛṣṇa and bestows *kṛṣṇa-bhakti.*

Śrī Pañca-tattva-praṇāma

pañca-tattvātmakaṁ kṛṣṇaṁ
bhakta-rūpa-svarūpakam
bhaktāvatāraṁ bhaktākhyaṁ
namāmi bhakta-śaktikam

I offer *praṇāma* to Śrī Caitanya Mahāprabhu in His five features as *bhakta, bhakta-rūpa, bhakta-svarūpa, bhakta-avatāra* and *bhakta-śakti.*

Pañca-tattva Mahā-mantra

śrī-kṛṣṇa-caitanya
prabhu nityānanda
śrī-advaita gadādhara
śrīvāsādi-gaura-bhakta-vṛnda

Mahā-mantra

hare kṛṣṇa hare kṛṣṇa
kṛṣṇa kṛṣṇa hare hare
hare rāma hare rāma
rāma rāma hare hare

Śrī Śrīmad Bhaktivedānta Nārāyaṇa Mahārāja

Śrī Śrīmad Bhaktivedānta Vāmana Mahārāja

Śrī Śrīmad A.C. Bhaktivedānta Swami Prabhupāda

Śrī Śrīmad Bhakti Prajñāna Keśava Gosvāmī

Śrī Prabandhāvalī

Chapter One

The Appearance Day of
Śrīla Bhaktivedānta Vāmana Mahārāja

Vyāsa is the personality who delineated the glories of the names, form, qualities and pastimes of Bhagavān in this world. The ceremony to honour the *ācārya* who, sitting on a throne in the service of Bhagavān, preaches His glories and attracts people towards Him is called Vyāsa-pūjā. Another name for Vyāsa-pūjā is *guru-pūjā*. In India, the general convention is that *guru-pūjā* is observed on the day of Guru-pūrṇimā. It is considered Vyāsa's appearance day, and on that day all *sampradāyas* worship their respective *gurus*. But in accordance with the scriptures, the primary *ācārya* of modern times, Śrī Śrīmad Bhaktisiddhānta Sarasvatī Gosvāmī Prabhupāda, established special worship of the *guru* on that *guru's* own specific appearance day. Real *guru-pūjā* is when, on his appearance day, the *guru* worships his whole *guru-paramparā* and instructs his disciples on how to do the same.

In the scriptures, the glories of the *guru* have been described extensively. Śrīla Viśvanātha Cakravartī Ṭhākura has written:

yasya prasādād bhagavat-prasādo
yasyāprasādān na gatiḥ kuto 'pi

Śrī Gurvaṣṭaka (8)

By the mercy of the *guru*, one receives the mercy of Bhagavān. And if one doesn't receive the mercy of the *guru*, he will never attain the *kṛpā* of Bhagavān. In *Śrīmad-Bhāgavatam* (11.17.27) Śrī Kṛṣṇa says:

ācāryaṁ māṁ vijānīyān
nāvamanyeta karhicit
na martya-buddhyāsūyeta
sarva-deva-mayo guruḥ

One should know the *guru* as the *āśraya-vigraha* and non-different from Me. One should never disrespect him or attribute faults to him by perceiving him with material vision, for he is the embodiment of all the demigods.

There are numerous demigods and goddesses, and amongst them Brahmā, Viṣṇu and Maheśa are primary. The *guru* is the embodiment of Brahmā, the embodiment of Viṣṇu, and also the embodiment of Maheśa. He is compared to Brahmā because just as Brahmā creates this world, the *guru* creates *bhakti* by sowing the seed of devotion in our hearts. Viṣṇu is the maintainer, and *gurudeva* is he who maintains our *bhakti*. As long as we haven't attained the stage of *prema*, he continues to strengthen our devotion. As conditioned souls, we cannot even imagine how much endeavour he makes for even one disciple. And as Maheśa is the destroyer, the *guru* destroys all of our *anarthas* and *aparādhas*. This is why the *guru* is said to be the embodiment of all the demigods.

There are so many *jīvas* in this world, and although some are inclined towards Bhagavān, most are averse to Him. Their intrinsic forms are as eternal servants of Kṛṣṇa, but forgetting this, they are wandering in material existence.

Without *bhakti* they will never possess any auspiciousness. Therefore sometimes Kṛṣṇa Himself descends into this world, sometimes He assumes different incarnations, and sometimes He sends His *śakti* in the form of the *guru*. Otherwise it would be impossible for the *jīvas* to ever receive auspiciousness. Only by *bhakti* can they attain their ultimate good fortune; yet *bhakti* is not a thing of this world. Inside the eternally perfected associates of Kṛṣṇa, the essence of the *saṁvit-* and *hlādinī-śaktis* is always present in the form of *prema-bhakti*. Until the *jīva* receives that essence, he will not possess any real auspiciousness. The *guru* is a resident of the spiritual world, and he descends into this world. He brings the *prema* of Goloka Vraja to this world and bestows it upon the conditioned souls. Such a great personality, an eternally perfected *rāgātmikā* devotee who possesses *vraja-prema* and brings it to this world, is known as a *śuddha-guru*.

As the current of the Gaṅgā carries water from the Himālayas down to the ocean, there is a current flowing through our *guru-paramparā* which, beginning from Kṛṣṇa Himself, has come down to the modern *ācāryas* and is presently flooding the entire material world with *kṛṣṇa-prema*. This is the primary function of the *guru*. If someone is not able to give this *prema*, then he is not really a *guru* at all. Being capable of bestowing *kṛṣṇa-prema* is the primary attribute of a genuine Vaiṣṇava *guru*.

Today is the appearance day of such a *guru*, Śrī Śrīmad Bhaktivedānta Vāmana Mahārāja, who serves as the present *ācārya* of the Śrī Gauḍīya Vedānta Samiti. He took birth in 1916 in the district of Jessore in East Bengal, which is now

Bangladesh. His boyhood name was Santoṣa, and his paternal uncle was one of Śrīla Bhaktisiddhānta Prabhupāda's first disciples, Nṛsiṁha Mahārāja. Vāmana Mahārāja's mother was also a disciple of Prabhupāda, and she was very strict; she would even discipline her husband. If her husband had been eating any prohibited food, she would not allow him to enter the house, and she disciplined the children in the same manner. Vāmana Mahārāja was the oldest of her four sons, and she was very concerned about him being influenced by his father. So when Vāmana Mahārāja was only nine years old, she took him to Prabhupāda's *maṭha* in Māyāpura where Nṛsiṁha Mahārāja was already staying. When they arrived there, Nṛsiṁha Mahārāja led them to our *gurudeva*, Śrīla Bhakti Prajñāna Keśava Mahārāja, who was the temple commander at that time. Residing in the *maṭha* from that day on, Vāmana Mahārāja received *harināma* initiation directly from Prabhupāda and has remained a lifelong *naiṣṭhika-brahmacārī*.

Our Guru Mahārāja immediately put Vāmana Mahārāja in school and would say to him, "I will give you some chocolate if you will recite just one *śloka* for me." In this way he learned many *ślokas*, and Gurudeva was always extremely affectionate to him. At that young age Vāmana Mahārāja learned how to seat Vaiṣṇavas for taking *prasāda* by giving them a leaf to eat from and some salt and water. And after all the Vaiṣṇavas had finished taking *prasāda* he would clean everything. He also learned how to cook there, and he could very quickly prepare first-class offerings.

After some time Prabhupāda departed from this world, and then our Guru Mahārāja established the Gauḍīya

Vedānta Samiti in 1943. I joined the mission in 1946, and at that time I saw how Vāmana Mahārāja was doing everything: writing letters, managing the temple, cooking, and travelling for preaching. Together with my godbrother Śrīla Trivikrama Mahārāja, we received *sannyāsa* from Guru Mahārāja on Gaura-pūrṇimā in 1954. Vāmana Mahārāja is a great scholar just as our *gurudeva* was. It has been said that he is like a dictionary of *ślokas* because he knows so many verses from the scriptures. When while lecturing Gurudeva would sometimes forget a *śloka*, Vāmana Mahārāja would always supply it from memory. Once, when we went to Āssām for preaching, Gurudeva boldly declared that the mouths of the people there who ate meat and fish were like the drains of sewers. One of the sects there was virtually prepared to stone us, and they challenged us by saying, "You say that Caitanya Mahāprabhu is Bhagavān Himself, but what evidence is there of this?" Guru Mahārāja turned to Vāmana Mahārāja and said, "Speak." Then Vāmana Mahārāja recited fifty *ślokas* one after the other from different scriptures as evidence, and those people were silenced.

Guru Mahārāja placed the entire responsibility of editing and publishing our Bengali magazine exclusively upon Vāmana Mahārāja. From his boyhood Vāmana Mahārāja studied *Bhāgavatam* verses and their commentaries, and as a result he can speak on Vaiṣṇava philosophy for hours without stopping. He is such a great scholar, and he is a very sweet person as well. With children he is very affectionate, and he speaks with them concerning things like ghosts that they enjoy hearing about. He attracts everyone to spiritual life, and even in an assembly of scholars, he is always the greatest scholar. He refutes others' misconceptions, but he does it in such a way that their feelings are not hurt, as if carefully performing a surgical operation.

Vāmana Mahārāja is very grave and quiet, and there is another special quality that he possesses: I have seen many people, myself included, who give explanations from the scriptures and enjoy taking praise from others for it. But having known Vāmana Mahārāja for almost fifty years, I have never seen him do this, not even by accident. He is also very tolerant. As if taking poison and digesting it, he may see the faults in others, but he never speaks about them. He has so much eagerness to preach the instructions of Caitanya Mahāprabhu, and he has preached in all the villages of West Bengal and Āssām. Bhagavān has especially empowered this great personality with many transcendental qualities. Today I pray to Śrīla Vāmana Mahārāja that he will mercifully allow me to always remain as his shadow, thereby enabling me to always follow him. I consider him to be my *śikṣā-guru*, because since the day I joined the mission he has given me whatever I required with great affection.

Chapter Two

The Disappearance Day of Śrīla A.C. Bhaktivedānta Swami Prabhupāda

Śrī Kṛṣṇa chose for His pure devotee, A.C. Bhaktivedānta Swami Mahārāja, to appear on the very auspicious day known as Nandotsava. This is the day after Janmāṣṭamī and the anniversary of the day on which Nanda Mahārāja held a great festival to celebrate Kṛṣṇa's birth. This fact alone signifies that Śrīla Swami Mahārāja was appearing for the purpose of performing some very important activities. His parents were very pious and therefore gave him the name Abhaya Caraṇa. *Abhaya* means "fearless", and *caraṇa* means "the lotus feet of the Lord", so Abhaya Caraṇa is a name of Kṛṣṇa because only Kṛṣṇa can grant real fearlessness in this world. Thus Swamijī was meant to give fearless shelter to the entire world. The giving of this name was very significant and nothing less than a divine arrangement.

I first met Swamijī in 1950 when I was staying with my *gurudeva* in our temple in Calcutta. Generally all devotees would show great respect to my *gurudeva*, but one day I saw Gurudeva himself show great respect to a householder devotee who had arrived from Allahabad. He spoke to him with great love and affection. At the first opportunity I asked my *gurudeva*, "Who is that devotee?" He replied, "He is Abhaya Caraṇāravinda. [Śrīla Bhaktisiddhānta

Sarasvatī] Prabhupāda gave him the title 'Bhaktivedānta', and although he is a *gṛhastha*, he is very learned, especially in English and Bengali. He is a very qualified devotee." Then, when Swamijī saw that I was rendering so much service to my *gurudeva*, he was attracted to me. He called me over and asked me where I was from, what my name was and so on.

When Swamijī first came to Mathurā, I personally requested him to take *sannyāsa*. He replied that when he was initiated by Prabhupāda, he was instructed to publish an English magazine and several books, and around the same time he read this verse from *Śrīmad-Bhāgavatam* (10.88.8):

yasyāham anugṛhṇāmi
hariṣye tad-dhanaṁ śanaiḥ
tato 'dhanaṁ tyajanty asya
svajanā duḥkha-duḥkhitam

[Śrī Kṛṣṇa said:] O King, when I favour someone, I gradually deprive him of all his wealth. In other words when a person, although desirous of giving up material sense gratification, is somehow engrossed in the sense objects present before him, he is afflicted with distress. For such a person the removal of these objects is itself a manifestation of My favour. When his wife, sons and relatives find him to be an abject failure beset with repeated misery, they reject the impoverished man.

Swamijī said to me, "For me, the meaning of this verse has come true. All of my business ventures failed, and my family turned against me. They used to say, 'You are a mad person. You are good for nothing and have spoiled everything.' So

I have spoiled everything, I am penniless, and now you are telling me that I should take *sannyāsa.*"

I used to joke with him, saying, "You desire to love your children and your wife, but they are not interested." I told him at that time that he should not endeavour any longer for these material concerns because Kṛṣṇa and Prabhupāda desired that instead he should do many very important things, like preach in Western countries. A few days after that, my *gurudeva* also came to Mathurā. I requested Gurudeva to persuade him to take *sannyāsa.* Swamijī and my *gurudeva* were very intimate friends who had lived together for some time. They were both intellectual giants from high-class families. Then Gurudeva called him and said, "Nārāyaṇa Mahārāja and all the boys here in the *maṭha* are saying that you should take *sannyāsa*, and I support them. It will be very beneficial." He agreed, saying, "The meaning of that verse from the *Bhāgavatam* has come directly upon my head, and now I must accept *sannyāsa.*" When the auspicious day for his initiation came, I personally prepared his outer cloth for *sannyāsa* and showed him how to wear it. I also prepared his *daṇḍa* and performed the *sannyāsa-yajña* with my own hands. Kṛṣṇa dāsa Bābājī Mahārāja was also present there, and as he led the congregational chanting of the *mahā-mantra* and I recited the *mantras* for the *yajña*, my *gurudeva* gave Swamijī the *sannyāsa-mantra.*

After that Swamijī and I spent a great deal of time together, first in Delhi and then at the Rādhā-Dāmodara Temple in Vṛndāvana. In those days he was mostly translating and writing. I saw at that time how he was *niskiñcana*, possessionless. He didn't even have a decent *cādar*, so I would give him mine to sit on and we would talk about Kṛṣṇa and how to do *bhajana*. We would also converse about Rūpa Gosvāmī and he would show me what he was writing. Then at midday we would make *capātīs* together – he would roll them and I would put them on the fire. He was so qualified in every respect. He was expert at playing the *mṛdaṅga*, performing *kīrtana* and *arcana*, writing, and giving lectures with word-for-word explanations of Sanskrit verses. He was always writing, chanting, and thinking about spiritual things, and he never wasted a moment.

He expressed to me his plan: "I will go to Western countries, start a hostel, and if necessary I will distribute eggs, meat and wine also, having full faith that by chanting the holy name of Kṛṣṇa, within a very few days Western people will abandon all these bad habits." Due to that faith and determination, in no time his mission was spread around the entire world. I have never seen an *ācārya* do anything like this before. Even Śaṅkarācārya took quite some time to spread his doctrine, and that was only in India. But in a very short time, from 1966 to 1977, he started so many centres for the worship of Śrī Rādhā-Kṛṣṇa, Caitanya Mahāprabhu and Jagannātha in Western countries, in India, in Eastern countries – everywhere. He not only established these centres, but he also attracted many thousands of very good boys and made them into scholars, *brahmacārīs* and *sannyāsīs*. As if with a magic wand he also attracted such qualified girls, ladies and children. He made true the prediction of Bhaktivinoda Ṭhākura that Westerners would one day take *tulasī-mālās* and mix with their Indian brothers, chanting, "Hare Kṛṣṇa, Hare Kṛṣṇa, Kṛṣṇa Kṛṣṇa, Hare Hare, Hare

Rāma, Hare Rāma, Rāma Rāma, Hare Hare."

Through the years he wrote me over one hundred letters from Western countries, describing how he was preaching and what he was doing. On his request I shipped all of his books to him from Delhi to America, and I also sent him *mṛdaṅgas*, *karatālas*, deities of Rādhā-Kṛṣṇa and many other items. He even wrote in one letter requesting me to send him a milksweet named Mathurā *peḍā*. He was very fond of this sweet, so I used to send it to him. And when he first returned from America to India, I was the first person to greet him at the airport.

There have been many preachers like Vivekānanda and others who went to Western countries, but they could not give what Swamijī has given there. They took only their own theories, but Svāmījī gave what Śrī Caitanya Mahāprabhu Himself wanted to give to this world, the holy name within *prema-sūtra*:[1]

nāma-prema-mālā gāṅthi' parāila saṁsāre

Śrī Caitanya-caritāmṛta (*Ādi-līlā* 4.40)

He wove a wreath of *harināma* and *prema* with which he garlanded the entire material world.

Caitanya Mahāprabhu was *mahā-vadānya*, the most munificent incarnation, and similarly, Rūpa Gosvāmī, Sanātana Gosvāmī, Jīva Gosvāmī, Raghunātha dāsa Gosvāmī, Kṛṣṇadāsa Kavirāja Gosvāmī, Viśvanātha Cakravartī Ṭhākura, Baladeva Vidyābhūṣaṇa and Bhaktivinoda Ṭhākura were all very munificent because

[1] This term means "an aphorism saturated with divine love", in other words the Hare Kṛṣṇa *maha-mantra*.

they distributed that which Mahāprabhu Himself wanted to give. Prabhupāda sent Swamijī to Western countries, knowing that he was a very great personality and that he could give what was within Prabhupāda's own heart. Vivekānanda and all of the other preachers went there and gave only these four things: *dharma* (religiosity), *artha* (economic development), *kāma* (sense gratification) and *mokṣa* (liberation). But they didn't really give even *mokṣa*, so they gave only three things. Some preachers may have tried to give *mokṣa* there also, but not *kṛṣṇa-prema*.

Because Swamijī had little time, he mostly emphasised *vaidhī-bhakti*. There are so many stages of *bhakti*, but ultimately *bhakti* means only *rāgānuga-bhakti*. He also wanted to preach in Western countries that which Rūpa Gosvāmī has given in *Ujjvala-nīlamaṇi*, and that which has been written by *ācāryas* like Raghunātha dāsa Gosvāmī and Kṛṣṇadāsa Kavirāja Gosvāmī, but he could not do it at that time. He had so little time, only ten or eleven years. So he tried to give *śraddhā*, then *niṣṭhā*, then *ruci*. We should know what *niṣṭhā* is. We are executing *śravaṇam*, *kīrtanam*, *viṣṇu-smaraṇam*, *pāda-sevanam*, *arcanam*, *vandanam*, *dāsyam*, *sakhyam* and *ātma-nivedanam*, as well as *nāma-kīrtana*, *sādhu-saṅga*, *bhāgavata-śravaṇa*, *mathurā-vāsa* and *śrī mūrti-sevā*, but we should go deeply into all of these activities. What is the meaning of *niṣṭhā*? When all *anarthas* are eradicated. And what are *anarthas*? Those things which entangle us in worldly intoxication. *Svarūpa-bhrama* (not knowing our real form), *asat-tṛṣṇā* (desire for temporary things), *hṛdaya-daurbalya* (weakness of heart), and *nāma-aparādha*, *vaiṣṇava-aparādha*, *sevā-aparādha* and *dhāma-*

aparādha – all these *anarthas* are mentioned in Viśvanātha Cakravartī Ṭhākura's *Mādhurya-kādambinī*. When all of a devotee's *anarthas* are eradicated, then *niṣṭhā* comes to him. Although we know that chanting the name of Kṛṣṇa and hearing about Kṛṣṇa are very beneficial, we do not possess the determination by which we can constantly perform these activities and steadily progress in *bhakti*. When one possesses such unwavering determination, it is called *niṣṭhā*. "I may die, but I cannot leave *kṛṣṇa-bhakti*" – this is *niṣṭhā*. And when we reach the stages of *ruci* and *āsakti*, it will seem that we simply cannot live without taking Kṛṣṇa's name or hearing *hari-kathā*.

There are two kinds of *śraddhā*: *vaidhī* and *rāgānugā*. Swamijī gave only *vaidhī-bhakti* because at that time it was not appropriate for him to explain *rāgānuga-bhakti*. He had written something of it in his books, but because most readers were not qualified enough to learn it at that time, he did not explain it in detail. But by practising *vaidhī-bhakti* we can eventually enter into *rāgānuga-bhakti*, which arises from that *śraddhā* which is full of "greed". Caitanya Mahāprabhu descended especially to give *sva-bhakti-śriyam*:

anarpita-carīṁ cirāt karuṇayāvatīrṇaḥ kalau
samarpayitum unnatojjvala-rasāṁ sva-bhakti-śriyam
hariḥ puraṭa-sundara-dyuti-kadamba-sandīpitaḥ
sadā hṛdaya-kandare sphuratu vaḥ śacī-nandanaḥ

Śrī Caitanya-caritāmṛta (*Ādi-līlā* 1.4)

May Śrī Śacīnandana Gaurahari, resplendent with the radiance of molten gold (having adopted the splendour of the limbs of Śrīmatī Rādhikā), forever manifest Himself within your hearts. He has descended in the age of Kali out of His causeless mercy to bestow upon the world that which had not been given for a long time, the most confidential wealth of His devotional service, the highest mellow of amorous love.

The meaning of this verse is very deep. Mahāprabhu came solely to give this, and Swamijī also came solely to give this. But first he had to prepare the soil for the seed, and so much time passed in doing that. He said that if the philosophies of *māyāvāda* or *advaitavāda* were not defeated first, then *bhakti* could not be established. He came to this world, as did Prabhupāda before him, to fulfil the mission of Caitanya Mahāprabhu, which is to bestow the *parakīya-bhāva* of Vraja. They did not come to give the *unnatojjvala-rasa* spoken of in this verse because that is the property of Śrīmatī Rādhikā alone. Caitanya Mahāprabhu descended to taste this, not to give it to others.

In this verse, the word *sva* means Śrīmatī Rādhikā, and *bhakti* means Her *prema*. Having stolen the inner *bhāva* and complexion of Śrīmatī Rādhikā, Kṛṣṇa Himself descended in Kali-yuga as Śacīnandana. Why is He known as Śacīnandana? Because He was very dear to His mother Śacī, and His mother was very humble and merciful. Rūpa Gosvāmī is saying in this verse that as the mother, being so merciful, gives her breast to her child, Caitanya Mahāprabhu has come to give *prema* to us. He is Kṛṣṇa in the form of Śrīmatī Rādhikā, and Rādhikā is also so merciful, even more than Kṛṣṇa. All of Kṛṣṇa's mercy is embodied in Rādhikā. So here, Śacīnandana means He who is extremely merciful. What did He give? He could not give the *mahābhāva* of Rādhikā because no one can taste the beauty of Kṛṣṇa, the sweetness of His form, and the sweetness of His pastimes as She does. Mahāprabhu wanted to taste only these things as She does, so what did He want to give? *Sva-bhakti-śriyam*: Śrīmatī Rādhikā is *sva-bhakti*, the *hlādinī* potency plus the *saṁvit* potency. Here the word *śrī* means *mañjarī*. So Rūpa Mañjarī, Anaṅga Mañjarī, Tulasī Mañjarī, Lavaṅga Mañjarī, Vinoda Mañjarī, Kamala Mañjarī, Nayana Mañjarī and all other *mañjarīs* are the *śrī* of Śrīmatī Rādhikā. In *Śrī Caitanya-caritāmṛta* it has been stated that Śrīmatī Rādhikā is the root creeper, and all the *gopīs* are the flowers, leaves and buds. When the wind blows, all of the buds and leaves will quiver. So if Kṛṣṇa and Rādhikā meet, and Rādhikā is in a very pleasing mood, then all of the leaves and buds are also pleased. If Kṛṣṇa draws any pictures on Her face or anywhere else on Her, all the *mañjarīs* will have those same designs on them. This is *bhakti-śriyam*, and Caitanya Mahāprabhu, Rūpa Gosvāmī, Prabhupāda and Swamijī all came solely to give this: *sva-bhakti-śriyam*, or *mañjarī-bhāva*.

But they all had to first prepare the soil by endeavouring to remove all of the weeds which are very harmful to that creeper. I have heard that Prabhupāda said he had come to this world solely to give *rādhā-dāsya*, but to accomplish this he had to do so much that his whole life was spent only in the preparatory work of cutting away the jungle, because at that time there was only *māyāvāda* philosophy here. Similarly, when Swamijī went to the Western countries, he faced much opposition from Christians. Many *ācāryas* went there, but their endeavours were not fruitful and Prabhupāda was not satisfied. But since Swamijī went, hundreds of thousands of editions of *Śrīmad-Bhāgavatam* have been published and distributed around the entire world.

In a very short time he accomplished all of this, but he really wanted to give *mañjarī-bhāva*, so we shouldn't be satisfied merely with what we received from him at that time. I feel that if he were present here today, he would be instructing us on *rāgānuga-bhakti*. He is omnipotent and he will inspire everything in our hearts as the *caitya-guru*. He is not far away from us; we should know that *gurudeva* is always with us. We should try to enter into the realm of this *rāgānuga-bhakti*, but we should not imitate. If we imitate, all will be ruined, so we must be careful not to behave as the *sahajiyās* do concerning *rāgānuga-bhakti*. In *Śrī Vilāpa-kusumāñjali*, Raghunātha dāsa Gosvāmī has prayed for the same *bhakti* that Viśvanātha Cakravartī Ṭhākura has prayed for in *Saṅkalpa-kalpadruma*. But we shouldn't try to go at once into that ocean of *govinda-līlāmṛta* – we'll be doomed. By thoughtfully executing *vaidhī-bhakti*, we will slowly but steadily enter into the realm of *rāgānuga-bhakti*. *Rāgānuga-bhakti* is the ultimate goal, but we should approach it very carefully by following the ordinary principles that Prabhupāda and Swamijī have taught.

Just before Swamijī departed this world, he begged my forgiveness for anything he may have said or written in the course of his preaching that may have offended me. For the same reason he also asked me to beg forgiveness from his godbrothers on his behalf. He said that he had brought many new devotees to the Gauḍīya line from Western countries. He said that since he was unable to give them everything in the short time he was present here, he wanted me to give them further instruction on *bhakti* and to always help them in any way I could. He also asked me to perform the ceremony to place him into *samādhi*.

I know that Śrīla A.C. Bhaktivedānta Swami Mahārāja was no ordinary devotee because, if he was, he would not have been able to preach all around the world the way he did in such a short period of time. I consider him my *śikṣā-guru*, and he always lives in the temple of my heart because I had such an intimate friendship with him. I think that he is always present here with us, and I pray to him that he will bestow mercy upon us so that we will all enter into *rāgānuga-bhakti* and *prema-bhakti* in this very lifetime.

Chapter Three

The Disappearance Day of Śrīla Bhakti Prajñāna Keśava Gosvāmī

Our Guru Mahārāja appeared in a family of landowners in the famous village of Banaripara in the district of Jessore in East Bengal. When he was born, his body was very soft and beautiful, and because he had a golden complexion, his mother and all the local ladies gave him the nickname Jonā (meaning "glow-worm"). His actual name was Bhīma. For approximately three or four months he didn't speak or cry at all, and his family was very worried. Then one day a Muslim mendicant who came to their home begging said to Gurudeva's mother, "Your son is not speaking?"

She replied, "How did you know that? If you can, please make him speak somehow."

The mendicant replied, "Do one thing. In the village there are some 'untouchables', persons from the *śūdra* class who work in the cremation grounds. They eat low-grade rice that is left soaking overnight. Beg some of this rice from them, feed it to your child, and then he will speak."

Guru Mahārāja's mother was a very hard-working lady, who mostly looked after their land. She would discipline her children very strictly, and they would never go anywhere without her permission. Everyone respected her. When she approached one of these *śūdra* families and asked for some of this rice, they said, "How can you take this? It has been touched by us!"

She replied, "Don't worry; just give me some of it." Obtaining some of this rice, she took it back to her home and put it before the child, and at once he started crying, "Mā! Mā!" and began speaking from that point on.

In his boyhood our *gurudeva* was very close to his father, who was especially affectionate towards him. At that time the people of East Bengal were very religious, and there would always be readings from *Bhagavad-gītā* and *Śrīmad-Bhāgavatam* going on. Then the Partition came, and it was as if the very heart of Bengal was torn out. From early childhood Gurudeva would grasp his father's finger and accompany him to religious programmes, and if it was dark, he would sit on his father's shoulders. Thus religious philosophy became his interest. There is a Hindi proverb, *honahāra viravāna ke hota cīkane pāta*, which means that when a sapling will grow to be fruitful, its leaves are very big and beautiful. Coming events cast their shadow, and from his childhood the symptoms were there that he would become a great personality.

As he grew up, he spent most of his time in the company of a great *mahātmā* who had an *āśrama* in the village. There he would hear readings from the *Gītā*, *Bhāgavatam* and Vedānta. When he was at school, at a very young age he started his own magazine, and its language was very literary. He was also an excellent speaker, and when he would speak in a large assembly, there would be no need of a loud-speaker. He didn't know as many *ślokas* as some devotees, but he would give such beautiful explanations. There is one verse from *Śrīmad-Bhāgavatam* (1.2.11) of which he would give an especially beautiful explanation:

vadanti tat tattva-vidas
tattvaṁ yaj jñānam advayam
brahmeti paramātmeti
bhagavān iti śabdyate

The *para-tattva* is *bhagavat-tattva*. From *brahma* there is Parabrahma, from *ātmā* there is Paramātmā, and from Viṣṇu there is Mahā-Viṣṇu. But for Svayam Bhagavān Kṛṣṇa there is no necessity of the words "Param Svayam Bhagavān", because Kṛṣṇa *is* the supreme *tattva*, and *brahma* and Paramātmā are His reflection and plenary portion, respectively. *Brahma* cannot actually be called an object, because any object must necessarily have qualities. *Brahma* is the potency of an object, and can be said to be the shelter of an object, but *brahma* itself is not an object. The names *brahma*, Paramātmā and Bhagavān are synonymous, but Bhagavān is to be worshipped, not *brahma*, because *brahma* is formless.

When I first joined the *maṭha*, I received such special mercy from Bhagavān that I had the opportunity to accompany our *gurudeva* to many big programmes where he would speak, and he always kept me with him. He gave my senior godbrother Śrīla Vāmana Mahārāja the responsibility for printing and, being a very qualified man, he has since printed many books and magazines one after the other. In order to help with the magazine and cooking, and to look after many services, Gurujī would keep me with him. His style of speaking and writing was wonderful, and it was my great fortune to hear so much from him. I always took notes and stayed with him like his shadow. Vāmana Mahārāja, just as now, was very quiet and didn't speak much, but my dear godbrother Trivikrama Mahārāja and myself were very talkative. We were always engaged in debating about this and that, and when Gurujī would become tired of us, he would say, "Take this book – the answer is there." These days devotees don't discuss topics of *tattva* much. Instead they speak about the type of clothing they wear and what kind of food they eat. When two Vaiṣṇavas meet, they should discuss *tattva*, and it was our great fortune to hear talks on *bhakti-tattva* from very learned devotees. But these days hardly anyone takes the time to discuss the meaning of the scriptures.

Gurujī was so intelligent and had so much potency in speaking that he could change yes to no and no to yes. It was amazing; without such devotees, preaching simply would not go on. If one of us wants to write and publish something, we have to look in many, many books and do so much editing, and even if five of us are working together, we still may have difficulty writing something. But what would Guru Mahārāja do? At the annual Navadvīpa *parikramā*, five to seven thousand devotees would come to offer *praṇāma* to him and he would speak with many of them. Somehow, in the midst of all this commotion, he would simultaneously dictate an article for his magazine to Vāmana Mahārāja. There would not even be any necessity to check it; at once it was ready to go to press. It was amazing how he would never have to look in any book. When one of us is preparing to speak something, we have to first look in so many books. And when we listen to someone speak or when we read something, we have to take notes in order to retain it. But Guru Mahārāja in his whole life never took any notes. He read so many books – his library is here in the *maṭha* [in Mathurā] – but he never took any notes. And he knew so much history; no *ācārya* knew more history than him. Śrīla Bhaktisiddhānta Prabhupāda called him a "Vedāntic *paṇḍita*".

Guru Mahārāja went from East Bengal to study at a very old and famous college near Calcutta. Many great scholars studied there and admission was not granted to everyone. But due to his superior intelligence he was awarded admission. In his very first year the dean and professors would call him to read *Śrī Caitanya-caritāmṛta* to them. *Caitanya-caritāmṛta* was composed in Bengali, but there is no Sanskrit book that can match its highly poetic and philosophical language.

jīvera 'svarūpa' haya – kṛṣṇera 'nitya-dāsa'
kṛṣṇera 'taṭasthā-śakti', 'bhedābheda-prakāśa'

Śrī Caitanya-caritāmṛta (*Madhya-līlā* 20.108)

The inherent form of the *jīva* is that of an eternal servant of Śrī Kṛṣṇa. The *jīva* is the marginal potency of Kṛṣṇa, and is therefore simultaneously one with and different from Him.

The dean and professors were unable to explain this verse. Even in our *sampradāya* you will find very few devotees who can properly explain it. So our *gurudeva* would have philosophical discussions with them, and in the end he left that college, saying, "Even the professors here understand nothing, so what will they teach me?" At that time Gandhi had started his movement to oppose the British government, saying, "The English must leave India; they will not impose the salt tax." All over India the people revolted against the British. So many big names like Balagangadhara Tilaka, Gorakle, C.R. Das, P.C. Raya and Lala Laja-patarai joined the opposition movement. It was as if the blood of India's youth was boiling, and at once all of India's industry stopped. Then the English thought, "Gandhi has so much influence?" Our *gurudeva* joined as well, but when Gandhi withdrew his movement due to violence, Gurujī along with many others joined the revolutionary party of Subash Candra Bose. Taking a knife and a rifle, he remained hidden within the forests and jungles for some time. At that time the British government issued a warrant for his arrest. He later joined the Gauḍīya Mission, and then ten years afterwards, the British government finally came to know of his whereabouts. One day some agents came to Māyāpura with a warrant for Gurujī's arrest, and they approached Prabhupāda about it. Prabhupāda told them, "But look how he has completely changed. He has become a *sādhu*, a *mahātmā*." After discussing the matter with Prabhupāda and considering further, they withdrew the warrant.

Gurujī was a champion footballer, and he was proficient in all subjects; he was an "all-rounder". He was proficient in sports, in studying, in fighting, in managing people and in speaking sweetly. At the age of only sixteen he was managing all the tenants on his father's land. He first came to the Caitanya Maṭha in Māyāpura at that age, and desired to receive *harināma* and *dīkṣā* from Prabhupāda. For some time he returned to his home and went to college, but at the age of eighteen he returned to the *maṭha* with his aunt. She was a very scholarly lady, and together they would compose very beautiful poems and essays. Once when they were conversing in Māyāpura, Prabhupāda said, "We will go on *parikramā* of the entire planet and establish one *maṭha* after the other. In England, America, and all of the holy places of India such as Haridwara, Prayāga, Vṛndāvana, Kāśī and South India, preaching will go on."

Then Gurujī's aunt said, "You are seeing a very big dream! You are like the poor man who begged a torn bag from someone, placed it under his head and fell asleep. While sleeping he dreamed, 'Oh, I am a millionaire! I am an emperor!' Who will see to all of this?"

Prabhupāda replied, "Vinoda[1] will see to it."

After this Guru Mahārāja began staying in the *maṭha* and did not return to his home again. He had all of the symptoms of a great personality on his body. His form was softer than butter, his arms extended down to his knees, and all auspicious signs were on his hands. He had "artist's fingers", very thin and long. In the morning he would eat just a little simple rice with some salt and then go out and work hard collecting donations for the *maṭha* all day. He would collect one *paisā* from each person, rather than taking a large amount from anyone. He would go to places where there were large crowds such as the bus and train stations, speak about Mahāprabhu's doctrine to people, and take just one *paisā* from each person. He would keep this money locked up in a box that had a slot on top for the coins, and the key

[1] Śrīla Keśava Mahārāja's *brahmacārī* name was Vinoda-bihārī Brahmacārī.

was left with Prabhupāda. He would do this every day until sunset, without even eating anything else.

One time Prabhupāda was being driven along in his car in Calcutta and he saw Vinoda resting under a tree with that money box placed under his head as a pillow. Tears came to his eyes and he said, "Such a beautiful young boy from a wealthy family, only eighteen years old; and for me, for the service of Bhagavān, he has left his parents and is undergoing such hardships?" When Gurudeva returned to the *maṭha* that night, Prabhupāda called him and said, "Vinoda, you were sleeping on the ground at Garimaṭa? You are undergoing so much hardship."

Gurujī replied, "No, this hardship is a matter of great happiness if only you will be satisfied with me. This is my everything. What more could I desire? If the *guru* is pleased, then Bhagavān is pleased. There is nothing greater than this."

Prabhupāda would call Gurujī "Tū" or "Tūi". There was only one other disciple for whom Prabhupāda used this affectionate name, and that was Paramānanda Prabhu, who was always with Prabhupāda. Gurujī was very intimate with Prabhupāda and would sleep only near him. Even if he went to take rest at one or two o'clock in the morning, he would knock on the door to Prabhupāda's room. The other devotees would complain, but Prabhupāda would always get up and open the door for him.

Once Guru Mahārāja was out collecting with Siddhasvarūpa Brahmacārī, who later became Śrīla Bhakti Śrīrūpa Siddhāntī Mahārāja. They had collected one large bag completely full with vegetables, and another half full. They got off the train at Howrah station, which was about five miles from the *maṭha*. There was no public transportation which covered the entire distance at that time, and there was no money available in the *maṭha* for taking a rickshaw. Gurudeva lifted up the full bag and said, "Let's go!" But Siddhāntī Mahārāja said, "No! You are my older brother and my *śikṣā-guru*. Therefore I will take the full bag!"

Gurujī replied, "No, you are a small boy, my younger brother. I will take it!" Snatching it back and forth from one another, finally Gurujī convinced Siddhāntī Mahārāja and carried that weight all the way to the *maṭha*. This is how he did *guru-sevā*. Whenever any necessity arose, Prabhupāda would say, "Where is Vinoda?"

After Guru Mahārāja's father passed away, his mother was crying for her son Vinoda day and night, even though she had three other sons in the house. One was a high school headmaster who later also became Prabhupāda's disciple and the *ācārya* of the Gauḍīya Mission, Śrīla Audulomī Mahārāja. He was fluent in English, and was a very talented speaker and writer. Vinoda was the youngest of the brothers. His mother sent a letter to Prabhupāda saying, "Please send Vinoda for some time to attend to some work here on our land, and when it is completed, he will return to you." There were some Muslim tenants who had refused to pay their rent for about five years, so Prabhupāda sent him there. Amongst the tenants there was one *guṇḍā* (hooligan) who was a very large man and the worst of them all. Gurujī ordered one of his family's hired workers to apprehend this man and bring him to the house. The man was beaten three or four times, and after this all the tenants began paying their rent.

On Prabhupāda's land in Māyāpura also there were Muslims who were not paying their rent. Prabhupāda was thinking to sell the land, but Gurujī pleaded with him to allow him to try and procure the rent money from these people. Prabhupāda said, "What will you do? You are only a boy of eighteen years." Eventually Prabhupāda agreed, and Gurujī had the ringleader apprehended, tied to a jack-fruit tree and beaten. Immediately all the tenants there became frightened and began paying their rent, and Gurujī offered that money as *puṣpāñjali* at the feet of Prabhupāda. But Gurujī would care for those people whom he respected more than he would for his own life. Everyone respected him like a father.

At the end of her life, Guru Mahārāja's mother sent another letter to Prabhupāda saying, "Please send my dear son Vinoda home for a little while." He called Vinoda and told him, "Your mother is dying; you must go to her immediately." Instead of going, Gurujī went and hid somewhere in the *maṭha* for a whole day and night. When Prabhupāda came to know of it, he sent for Gurujī and told him, "Your mother is very ill. You should go to her. I instructed you to go, so why haven't you gone?"

Guru Mahārāja replied, "Prabhu, after so many births I have attained the shelter of your feet. By your mercy, I have finally come to *bhagavad-bhakti* after so many births. Suppose I go to my mother, and while she is taking her last breath she places her hand on my head and says to me, 'I am going now. Who will look after our property? You must do it.' What will I do then? Having left your lotus feet, I will again be trapped in *māyā*." Falling at Prabhupāda's feet, he began crying, and Prabhupāda bestowed plentiful blessings upon him. Until one's determination is like this, he does not have the qualification to leave his home and family. One must have the understanding of a *madhyama-adhikārī* that the bodily relations of this material world are meaningless. Otherwise, even without being requested, one will automatically return to his home and family. And if he does continue to stay in the *maṭha*, it will only be for procuring money, women and prestige. He will have only gone in a circle and will end up back where he started. Therefore one cannot leave his home and family until he has this qualification.

There was a disciple of Prabhupāda named Rāma-govinda Vidyāratna, who was a scholar of Vedānta, the *Bhāgavatam* and all the scriptures. He was a very good devotee and later became Naimi Mahārāja. Once, he desired to have *darśana* of Prabhupāda's *guru*, Śrīla Gaura-kiśora dāsa Bābājī Mahārāja, and Gurujī also wanted to go; so taking Prabhupāda's permission, they went. At that time, to avoid the trouble that ordinary people were giving him, Bābājī Mahārāja had locked himself in a latrine for about a week and was just chanting, "Hare Kṛṣṇa, Hare Kṛṣṇa..." The news reached the district magistrate and the police superintendent, and at once they all came running there. Seeing that the door was locked from inside, they approached with folded hands and said, "Bābājī Mahārāja, we will construct you a very nice hut for *bhajana*."

He replied, "No, this is very nice."

"Why?"

"Because the stench of the lust of materialistic people does not come here. I prefer the stench of stool to that."

"Alright, Mahārāja, we will supply you with one boy to keep those people away from you." Day and night they were trying to persuade him to come out, but he would only say, "For me, this is Vaikuṇṭha." So many times they asked him to please open the door, but time and again he would reply, "I am not well; I am unable to do it." He would not open the door for those people, and he just continued chanting "Hare Kṛṣṇa, Hare Kṛṣṇa, Kṛṣṇa..." Then Gurujī approached the door and said, "Bābājī Mahārāja, we are disciples of Bhaktisiddhānta Sarasvatī." Hearing the name of Prabhupāda, Bābājī Mahārāja at once stood up. Opening the door, he let them in and again locked the door. The two boys offered *praṇāma* and, grasping the feet of Bābājī Mahārāja, Gurujī said, "Please give us your blessings." Then Bābājī Mahārāja told him, "I will take all of your hardships and impediments away so you can always perform *bhajana* freely – this is my blessing." Later on, Gurujī would say on many occasions that although difficulties may have come to him from time to time, by the mercy of Bābājī Mahārāja, nothing could ever disturb him.

Chapter Four

The Disappearance Day of Śrīla Bhaktisiddhānta Sarasvatī Prabhupāda

Today is the anniversary of the day of separation from *nitya-līlā praviṣṭa oṁ viṣṇupāda aṣṭottara-śata* Śrī Śrīmad Bhaktisiddhānta Sarasvatī Gosvāmī Prabhupāda. It is the day of *pañcamī*, and he also appeared on *pañcamī*. He took birth in the home of Bhaktivinoda Ṭhākura, who is an eternal associate of both Śrī Kṛṣṇa and Śrī Caitanya Mahāprabhu. Just as the sage Bhagīratha brought the Gaṅgā to this world, Bhaktivinoda Ṭhākura was the great personality who brought the current of *bhakti* to this world in the modern era. When the so-called *gosvāmīs* were making a business out of *bhakti* while engaging in varieties of worldly enjoyment, when in the name of Mahāprabhu so many kinds of bogus philosophies were prevalent, such as *sakhī-bekī*, *smārta-jāti*, *sahajiyā*, etc. – at that time Śrīla Bhaktivinoda Ṭhākura came. After that, Prabhupāda appeared in the form of his son, Bimalā Prasāda. If these two great personalities had not appeared, then *śuddha-bhakti* would not exist in the world today. And from the time that they disappeared, society began reverting back to its previous condition. At first there were thirteen known *sahajiyā* cults, then our Guru Mahārāja, Śrīla Bhakti

Prajñāna Keśava Gosvāmī, counted thirty-nine. And how many there are now, no one knows.

I am also seeing how things are gradually changing. We saw how renounced the devotees were before. For instance, we never used to see socks on the feet of any Vaiṣṇava, and we never saw devotees wearing such sweaters and *cādaras* as we do now. They only wore the bare necessities of clothing and a cheap blanket, even as they attended *maṅgala-ārati* in the morning cold. It is only after the disappearance of Prabhupāda that devotees can be seen to wear these other things. They would live with such simplicity, eating only *śāk*, rice and a thin dahl, but in comparison to them, just look at the way we are living! And I speak for myself also – their knowledge, their renunciation and their spiritual conception were of such a high standard that in comparison to them we are so inferior.

The period between Viśvanātha Cakravartī Ṭhākura and Bhaktivinoda Ṭhākura was an age of darkness for Gauḍīya Vaiṣṇavism. Living at that time were some real Vaiṣṇavas who performed real *bhajana*, but mostly, just as we still see sometimes today, the so-called Vaiṣṇavas only performed rituals for wages. When someone would die, people would call the Gauḍīya Vaiṣṇava *bābājīs*, who would come and chant some ceremonial *kīrtana* and perform other rituals for wages. And there was so much misconduct in their behaviour. Seeing this, Bhaktivinoda Ṭhākura thought, "These people are Vaiṣṇavas? The conception of Mahāprabhu has completely vanished. What can be done?" He was very worried. Bhaktivinoda Ṭhākura endeavoured to his utmost, but changes did not come about in his lifetime to the degree that he would have liked. He went from town to town and village to village inaugurating the *nāma-haṭṭa*. In each village he would assemble four or five of the religious men, form a committee and hold programmes for *harināma-kīrtana* on Sundays. Gradually it spread from one village to the next, but overall his preaching was limited to Navadvīpa, Calcutta and the rest of Bengal.

He published the magazine *Sajjana-toṣaṇī*, and through its medium he gradually published *Śrī Caitanya-caritāmṛta* and other books in instalments. He made a circle of devotees, and also revealed Navadvīpa-dhāma through his writings, although the scholars of society and the *sahajiyās* didn't accept his ideology. Then Prabhupāda appeared in Purī. Because Bhaktivinoda Ṭhākura was a district magistrate, he would be transferred here and there, but he would always keep *Bhakti-rasāmṛta-sindhu* and *Caitanya-caritāmṛta* with him and explain them to his son. Prabhupāda received so much instruction from him, but we should understand that Prabhupāda is an eternally liberated soul; there was no one in the world like him. Without being educated in school or college he learned all subjects very quickly and became a great scholar in Sanskrit. His English was so high that even professors of English could not understand it. I have been told by some learned Western devotees that when reading his *Brahma-saṁhitā*, they must repeatedly consult the dictionary. And his Bengali was also of such a high standard that even eminent scholars found it difficult to follow. He said that spiritual language should be like that; it shouldn't be so simple to understand. As one progresses spiritually by remaining in the company of Vaiṣṇavas, he will be able to understand spiritual vernacular.

At the age of seven or eight, Prabhupāda began worshipping a deity of Kūrmadeva, and Bhaktivinoda Ṭhākura gave him the *mahā-mantra* and other *mantras* for his *pūjā*. At the age of eighteen, all of the scholars of astronomy in Bengal gave him the title "Sarasvatī". After that he attended college but quarrelled with the professors, saying, "Will I learn from you, or teach you?" When he abandoned his studies, Bhaktivinoda Ṭhākura and other family members became concerned, so they took him to Purī where he began studying at Satāsana Āśrama, which is where Svarūpa Dāmodara and Raghunātha dāsa Gosvāmī had lived. Vaiṣṇavas used to regularly meet there, and now Śrīla Siddhāntī Mahārāja has a *maṭha* at that very place. There Prabhupāda began giving readings from *Caitanya-caritāmṛta*. Present there were some *bābājīs* who considered themselves *rasika*, and when they heard Prabhupāda's explanations, they became inimical to him. Seeing this, Bhaktivinoda Ṭhākura took him away from there and had him begin teaching the son of the king of Tripura.

Prabhupāda had a great library of Vaiṣṇava literature, and having read through it thoroughly, he began teaching the son of the king in such a way that the boy accepted a chanting *mālā* and began wearing *tilaka*. He became detached from the world, and gradually, hearing *hari-kathā* became his sole interest. Seeing this, the queen became very annoyed and said to the king, "This boy will become useless! Then, after your demise, what will happen? Who will make offerings to our departed souls? He will become a renunciate, and everything will be ruined! Quickly get rid of this teacher. Give him four hundred rupees to go – we don't need money, we need a son!" That was approximately one hundred years ago, so you can imagine how much four hundred rupees was worth then. The queen put so much pressure on her husband that in the end he approached Prabhupāda and very humbly said, "It is a matter of great unhappiness that our family members are not in favour of you; they are afraid that the boy will take up *bhakti* and become a renunciate. I consider that it has been our great good fortune to have met a person like you and had our son educated by you, but the others don't understand." The king approached Bhaktivinoda Ṭhākura and offered the money to him, but without accepting it they left there.

Then Bhaktivinoda Ṭhākura started a homeopathic shop. When the shop was unsuccessful, he thought, "I was not made to run a shop anyway," and he went and purchased some land in Māyāpura. After locating the birthplace of Mahāprabhu, he installed deities there of Gaura, Viṣṇupriyā and Lakṣmīpriyā, as well as small Rādhā-Kṛṣṇa *mūrtis*. After Bhaktivinoda Ṭhākura's disappearance, Prabhupāda was determined to follow the Navadvīpa-dhāma *parikramā* that his father had written, and to attract people he invited great *kīrtana* performers to attend. He set up a large tent, thousands of people came for the *parikramā*, and there the *kathā* of *śuddha-bhagavad-bhakti* commenced.

Gradually, qualified youths of only sixteen, seventeen and eighteen years, whose hearts were soft and pure, came forward, and Prabhupāda made them into *brahmacārīs* and *sannyāsīs*. With great ease he was able to train them, but those who were over fifty years old, like parrots could not be taught anything new. Then devotees like our Guru Mahārāja, Bon Mahārāja, Bhakti Pradīpa Tīrtha Mahārāja, Bhakti Vilāsa Tīrtha Mahārāja, Araṇya Mahārāja and Narahari Prabhu came. In the beginning there in Māyāpura, Narahari Prabhu would offer *ārati* while Prabhupāda played the hand-held gong, and gradually the preaching started. The convention of *tridaṇḍi-sannyāsa* was established, and the result is that today the name and conception of Caitanya Mahāprabhu are being vigorously preached. Within eleven years, from 1926–37, preaching was spread everywhere, but before that, so much time was spent in merely setting the foundation. Prabhupāda published many magazines – daily, weekly, monthly – in the Sanskrit, Bengali, Hindi, Orissan, English and Assamese languages, and very easily we have all inherited the fruit of his endeavour. He established the Gauḍīya line very strictly with great endeavour, and there were so many difficulties in his preaching campaign that we cannot even imagine them. There was so much opposition to Prabhupāda's preaching at that time that his disciples were not even allowed to enter the *mandiras* in Vṛndāvana or Navadvīpa.

Prabhupāda began culturing the creeper of devotion by cutting off all of the unnecessary branches and sub-branches. How? First of all he revised the *guru-paramparā*. He said that we are of Mahāprabhu's line, and he removed the names of those who were not fully perfected. After establishing the names of Brahmā, Nārada and Vyāsa, he went straight to Madhva. Prabhupāda accepted the names of those from whom the people of this world would get the most benefit, and mostly they were *brahmacārīs*. For the most part he didn't accept the names of those who had been *gṛhasthas* for a long time. After Madhva, he recognised some special personalities, and then he went to the name of Mādhavendra Purī. Everyone accepts him, and then from him there is Īśvara Purī, Svarūpa Dāmodara, the Six Gosvāmīs, and then Kṛṣṇadāsa Kavirāja Gosvāmī. At this point some had divided into the lines of Nityānanda Prabhu, Advaita Ācārya, Gadādhara Paṇḍita, Vakreśvara Paṇḍita, Lokanātha Gosvāmī and others, but Prabhupāda said, "We accept in our line those who are fully perfected souls, who know the correct *siddhānta* and who are *rasika*, wherever they are." In this way all of the various lines were represented in our *paramparā* in one place or another.

There are so many lines of disciplic succession, but Prabhupāda said that we will recognise the *guru-paramparā*, not the disciplic succession. The *guru-paramparā* is composed solely of those who were *bhāgavata-gurus*, even if they made no disciples and there is therefore no direct disciplic line coming from them. Some of them may not have initiated any disciples at all, but still they are *jagad-gurus*. In this way, with all-pervading vision he collected all the *mahājanas* and made what is known as the *bhāgavata-paramparā* or *guru-paramparā*.

After the departure of Viśvanātha Cakravartī Ṭhākura, so many familial disciplic lines arose, but Prabhupāda ignored them and gave recognition to Baladeva Vidyābhūṣaṇa, and then Jagannātha dāsa Bābājī. He accepted only those in whom he detected the real spiritual *siddhānta*. Simply receiving the *mantra* in one's ear and wearing a *dhotī* or other cloth given by the *guru* does not qualify one as the *guru's* successor. Bhaktivinoda Ṭhākura did not receive any *mantra* from Jagannātha dāsa Bābājī Mahārāja, so how was he his disciple? He was a disciple of his conception: his feelings towards Kṛṣṇa, his conception of *rasa* and his conception of *tattva*. This is a disciple. Most people can't understand this, but being able to see with such insight, Prabhupāda declared this to be our line. Gaura-kiśora dāsa Bābājī Mahārāja was also not an initiated disciple of Bhaktivinoda Ṭhākura, but he embraced all of Bhaktivinoda Ṭhākura's sentiments and conceptions, and due to this his name appears next in the succession. At this point, all of the *bābājīs* said, "Whose disciple is Bhaktisiddhānta Sarasvatī? Who gave him *sannyāsa*? Why doesn't he wear the same cloth as Sanātana Gosvāmī did? In our *sampradāya*, after Nityānanda Prabhu and Svarūpa Dāmodara, everyone wore white cloth, but we see that he wears saffron cloth and has accepted a *daṇḍa*. How can he do this?" But what relation does wearing either orange or white cloth have with *bhakti*? Is there any relation?

kibā vipra, kibā nyāsī, śūdra kene naya
yei kṛṣṇa-tattva-vettā, sei 'guru' haya

Śrī Caitanya-caritāmṛta (*Madhya-līlā* 8.128)

Whether one is a *brāhmaṇa*, a *sannyāsī* or a *sūdra*, if he knows *kṛṣṇa-tattva*, then he is a *guru*, so what to speak of being a Vaiṣṇava? Prabhupāda was thinking, "We are not qualified to accept the dress that was worn by such great personalities as Rūpa, Sanātana, Jīva and Kṛṣṇadāsa Kavirāja. We will remain in the ordinary dress of *sannyāsīs* and will not accept the dress of *paramahaṁsa-bābājīs*. Remaining within the *varṇāśrama* system as *brahmacārīs* and *sannyāsīs*, we will keep the ideal of that *paramahaṁsa* dress above our heads. Otherwise, if we accept that dress and commit sinful activities, it will be *aparādha* at the feet of Rūpa and Sanātana." Some *bābājīs* criticised him for training *brahmacārīs* and giving them the sacred thread, but our Guru Mahārāja said that those *bābājīs* were all fools, like animals. They wore *paramahaṁsa* dress and gave the elevated *gopī-mantra* to anyone and everyone who came, yet Prabhupāda was only training *brahmacārīs* and giving them instructions on how to control the senses – so which is correct? First Prabhupāda wanted us to understand what is *siddhānta*, i.e. *jīva-tattva*, *māyā-tattva* and *bhagavat-tattva*, and how to avoid *māyā* in the forms of *kanaka* (wealth), *kāminī* (women) and *pratiṣṭhā* (prestige) – these are the beginning instructions. *Gopī-bhāva* is very elevated; first we must understand that "I am *kṛṣṇa-dāsa*" and begin taking *harināma*. But these *bābājīs* immediately give their conception of *gopī-bhāva* to whoever approaches them; then they all chant "I am a *gopī*, I am a *gopī*" and in this way create a disturbance in society.

Every morning in our *maṭha* we sing the song in which Prabhupāda established the *bhāgavata-paramparā*: *kṛṣṇa haite catur-mukha*... In his composing of this song, he accepted all of the great, perfected personalities from different lines and declared, "This is the line of Gaura." If Prabhupāda had not come, then today would the name of Mahāprabhu and talks from *Bhagavad-gītā* and *Śrīmad Bhāgavatam* be found anywhere? Here in Mathurā, in Vraja and everywhere else, *gaura-kīrtana* and *hari-kathā* are still going on and have not vanished. Therefore the world will forever remain indebted to Prabhupāda for his preaching. He never approached wealthy people, but he would take one *paisā* from each person he met. And our Guru Mahārāja did the same. Although he was from a wealthy family, he would take a wooden box with a slot in it into the market and also onto the trains, trams and buses. He would speak with people from all classes, and in this way the preaching spread in all directions. We should also engage in such a pure form of preaching, and not just remain idle after hearing this. As if giving an injection, you should all encourage others to start taking *harināma* and hearing this conception, whether you are a man or lady, married or unmarried. And don't think that because one is not educated he cannot do it. Did Haridāsa Ṭhākura have any college degree? Did Raghunātha dāsa Gosvāmī and others? But their activities were first class, and their conceptions were extremely high.

We are regularly hearing *tattva* from scriptures such as *Śrīmad-Bhāgavatam* and *Bṛhad-bhāgavatāmṛta*, but how will others also get the opportunity to hear it? After hearing it we should take it to many other people, and this is the duty of each and every one of us. With great love we should take *harināma* and encourage others to chant it. We should hear *siddhānta* ourselves and then help others to understand it; that will give Prabhupāda great pleasure. To the very end of his life Prabhupāda said, "We are mere labourers; we are the peons of *bhagavat-kathā*." He never made himself a permanent living situation in an opulent temple, but always kept moving. These days we do things a little differently, but we should always try to follow not only Prabhupāda's philosophical conception but the ideal he showed through his own behaviour as well.

These ideas serve as the very foundation of *bhakti*, and if this foundation is not established, then we will fall from hearing the higher levels of *kathā*. For instance, Bhaktivinoda Ṭhākura has written a song entitled *Vibhāvarī Śeṣa*, which includes lines such as:

yāmuna-jīvana, keli-parāyaṇa,
mānasa-candra-cakora
nāma-sudhā-rasa, gāo kṛṣṇa-yaśa,
rākho vacana mana mora

Śrī Kṛṣṇa is the life of the Yamunā, He is always engaged in amorous pastimes and He is the moon of the *gopīs'* hearts. Sing the glories of He whose name is pure *rasa* – O mind, always remember these words.

In our *maṭha* we sing this every day, and there is certainly some benefit in it, but do we understand the complete *bhāva* contained within it? Nothing remains outside these lines – not the *rāsa-līlā*, not the *Bhramara-gīta*, not the *Veṇu-gīta*, nothing. Everything is there, and all of the previous lines of this song are similarly saturated with both *rasa* and *tattva*. *Phula-śara-yojaka kāma* – what is the meaning? The complete *kāma-gāyatrī* has come here. *Śara* means an arrow, an arrow of *kāma* (desire) which Kṛṣṇa places on His bow. How many of these arrows does Kṛṣṇa have? Five: His sidelong glances and His eyebrows, cheeks, nose and smile. So tell me, is there anything remaining outside these lines?

Helping the people of the world to understand these topics is the real task of the *guru-paramparā* – those who are conversant with *rasa*, the *dīkṣā*- and *śikṣā-gurus*. If we examine one line of this song after another, then for so many days so many lectures could be given, and our hearts would become full of *rasa* and divine bliss upon hearing their full meaning. So much *bhāva* has been put into each word by Bhaktivinoda Ṭhākura, and it is the same with the compositions of Narottama Ṭhākura and Viśvanātha Cakravartī Ṭhākura. To understand what our *ācāryas* have given, great intelligence and *bhāva* are required. And if we have such a *bhāva* in our hearts by which we can understand the poetry and the special characteristics of *ācāryas* like Prabhupāda, then wherever we may go, it will always remain with us.

In explaining the line *paraṁ vijayate śrī-kṛṣṇa-saṅkīrtanam* from the first verse of Mahāprabhu's *Śikṣāṣṭaka*, Prabhupāda wrote that this is the Gauḍīya Maṭha's mode of worship. There are three stages: the beginning stage of *sādhana*, the intermediate stage of *bhāva*, and the final attainment produced by that *bhāva*, which is called *prema*. *Sādhana* is that practice by which *śuddha-sattva-bhāva* arises, and if it does not arise, what one is practising cannot be called *sādhana*. We can all examine ourselves and see if we are practising the *sādhana* that makes *bhāva* arise or not. Are the symptoms there, or not? We may not even have the proper aim in our *sādhana*. If someone is striking a match, what is his aim? To obtain a flame; and if after striking one match a flame is not obtained, then he will take another match and try again. Our endeavour to reach the *sādhya* (final attainment) through the practice of *sādhana* is like that. *Kṣud-anuvṛtti* (spiritual "hunger"), *tuṣṭi* (satisfaction) and *puṣṭi* (strength)

– these three things should appear, and if they don't, then we are not really practising *sādhana* and cannot be called real *sādhakas*. Whatever we do should be done with this vision: "By performing this activity, *bhāva* for Kṛṣṇa will arise." Is the match producing a flame or not? If we see that our *sādhana* is producing attachment for material results such as *pratiṣṭhā*, then we are moving in the wrong direction. Therefore we should understand this point well: the sole aim of *kīrtana* is to make *bhāva* arise.

Ceto-darpaṇa-mārjanam: in our practice of *nāma-saṅkīrtana*, have our minds become purified or not? Are our minds going towards wealth, material enjoyment and prestige? Do we consider material enjoyment to be poisonous or favourable to us? Material enjoyment is poison. Haridāsa Ṭhākura was taking *harināma* in a solitary place when a very beautiful woman approached him and said, "Prabhu, you will no longer have to cook for yourself. You won't have to fetch water, and I will also serve your *tulasī* plant. You can just chant *harināma* all day and I will perform all of your tasks. And if you become fatigued, I will massage your feet." But did Haridāsa Ṭhākura accept her?

All types of material enjoyment should be understood to be poison, whether one is a man or a woman. If we consider things like luxurious food and accommodation to be favourable to us, then the mirror of the mind will not be cleansed and the reflection of one's own spiritual form will not be visible. The mirror should be made pure; there should be no dust or anything on it. We should be able to see what is our illusory body, what is our spiritual body and what all of our faults are; but it is our great misfortune that instead we only see others' faults. The first type of contamination affecting our minds is thinking that we are the material body. We are eternal servants of Kṛṣṇa, but the most prevalent dust on the mirror of the mind is thinking that we are the material body. Endeavouring for the happiness of the body is dust on the mirror, or contamination on our minds.

There are so many *anarthas*: *svarūpa-bhrama* (bewilderment concerning one's actual form and nature), *asat-tṛṣṇā* (desire for temporary things), *hṛdaya-daurbalya* (weakness of heart) and *aparādha* (offences). Besides these, described in Viśvanātha Cakravartī Ṭhākura's *Mādhurya-kādambinī*, are *utsāhamayī* (false confidence), *ghanataralā* (sporadic endeavour), *vyūḍha-vikalpā* (indecision), *viṣaya-saṅgarā* (combat with the senses), *niyamākṣamā* (inability to uphold vows) and *taraṅga-raṅgiṇī* (delighting in the material facilities produced by devotion).

Then there are four types of *aparādha*: *duṣkṛtottha* (arising from previous sins), *sukṛtottha* (arising from previous piety), *aparādhottha* (arising from offences in chanting) and *bhaktyuttha* (arising from imperfect service). When all of these are eradicated, then our real selves, the *ātmā*, will reflect in the mirror of the mind; but for now our vision is distorted. We consider the pain and happiness of the material body to be our own, and our worldly relations and worldly loss and gain to be related to our very selves. *Bhava-mahā-dāvāgni-nirvāpaṇaṁ*: this is the forest fire of material existence in which we are time and again taking birth.

When the mirror of the mind is purified, then this great

fire will be extinguished and we will progress along the path of *sādhana* for *uttama-bhakti*, that devotion which is free from any tendencies towards *karma* or *jñāna*. That devotion will be *kleśa-ghnī*, that which burns away so many types of difficulties. It will not happen all at once, but gradually. First there is *śraddhā*, then *niṣṭhā*, and then we will move towards *ruci* and *āsakti* when our *anarthas* will have been mostly eradicated. However, those *anarthas* may still exist in root form. One may shave his head, but has even one hair completely disappeared? Its roots are still there, and hair will again appear after a couple of days. In the same way, when we have reached the stage of *āsakti*, only the roots of *anarthas* will remain; externally they will not be visible. If a favourable environment is given to them – that is, if we keep bad company or offend a Vaiṣṇava – then they will reappear. But upon reaching the stage of *bhāva*, they will be finished forever.

Then there is *śubhadā*, which is of many varieties. In the worldly sense, *śubha* means having wealth, good progeny, position, fame and knowledge, and keeping the body healthy so that the effects of old age will not come prematurely. But what is real *śubha*? Having *ruci* for the name and *līlā-kathā* of Bhagavān and for the limbs of *bhagavad-bhajana-sādhana*. Having eagerness for these things is *śubha*, and that *śubha* is the lotus flower described by the words *śreyaḥ-kairava-candrikā-vitaraṇam*. If the rays of the moon fall upon it, it will bloom purely and without blemishes. How will such pure *bhakti* arise in the heart? The *śakti* of *harināma* is like the rays of the moon which make the lotus of the heart gradually bloom, taking it through the stages of *niṣṭhā*, *ruci*, *āsakti* and *bhāva*. When it fully blossoms, that is the stage of *prema*. But for the *śakti* of *harināma* to act in this way, our interest must be drawn away from material life. In the same way as two swords will not remain together in one scabbard, *māyā* and *bhakti* will not remain together in one's heart.

Vidyā-vadhū-jīvanam: *nāma-saṅkīrtana* is the very life of *vidyā-vadhū*. *Vidyā* is that by which we can know *jīva-tattva*, *māyā-tattva*, and ultimately Kṛṣṇa; it does not mean knowledge of mundane science or how to make money. Real *vidyā* is *bhakti* and ultimately assumes the form of the *vadhū*, or consort, of Kṛṣṇa. First there is *sādhana-bhakti*, then *bhāva-bhakti*, and finally *prema-bhakti*. After entering *prema-bhakti*, one's devotion develops through the stages of *sneha*, *māna*, *praṇaya*, *rāga*, *anurāga*, *bhāva* and finally *mahābhāva*. The embodiment of *mahābhāva* is Śrīmatī Rādhikā, who is the *vadhū*, or consort, of Kṛṣṇa. Over and above the *sandhinī-śakti*, the *saṁvit-* and *hlādinī-śaktis* fully manifest as *rādhā-bhāva*. This is *vidyā-vadhū*, and if even one ray of this transcendental potency enters into our hearts, it is called *bhāva*.

Ānandāmbudhi-vardhanaṁ prati-padam: if we are chanting *harināma* with this *bhāva*, then with every step we will experience increasing *ānanda*, divine joy. In the *mahā-mantra*, there is *kṛṣṇa-nāma* and also Hare, which means She who attracts Kṛṣṇa away to the *kuñja*, Śrīmatī Rādhikā. This *bhāva* is so deep that it has no end, and this is the *nāma*, so saturated with *rasa*, that Caitanya Mahāprabhu brought to this world. When we chant the *mahā-mantra* with this *bhāva*, then every step will submerge us deeper into the ocean of divine bliss. *Pūrṇāmṛtāsvādanam* – what is *pūrṇāmṛta*, the complete nectar? *Prema*, and one will perpetually relish it. Absorbed in chanting the name in this way, our *ācāryas* such as Jayadeva Gosvāmī, Sanātana Gosvāmī and Bhaktivinoda Ṭhākura could envision divine pastimes and compose such nectarean literatures. And *sarvātma-snapanam* – one will never desire to resurface from that ocean of nectar where there is not even a trace of *māyā*, meaning that they have entered into *svarūpa-siddhi*. This is the explanation of the first verse of Mahāprabhu's *Śikṣāṣṭaka* given by Śrīla Bhaktisiddhānta Sarasvatī Prabhupāda, whose return to Śrī Rādhā-Kṛṣṇa's eternal pastimes we are commemorating on this day.

Chapter Five

The Disappearance Day of Śrīla Gaura-kiśora dāsa Bābājī Mahārāja

We cannot touch Śrīla Gaura-kiśora dāsa Bābājī Mahārāja's renounced lifestyle and high standard of *bhajana*, but we can at least accept and follow whatever lower principles that he established for us and practised in his own life. After making sufficient spiritual progress, we may be able to accept the higher things, but we should not desire to follow them in our present condition. Who can possibly follow his extreme renunciation, such as eating the clay of the Yamunā and Rādhā-kuṇḍa and remaining completely dependent on Bhagavān? He felt that if he lived in a *mandira* many people would come and disrupt his *bhajana*, so instead he lived in a latrine. People would come seeking his blessings for the purpose of attaining some material benefit, but he considered the stench of the latrine to be preferable to the stench of those people's words. For us this is impossible, even for one minute. Therefore a *kaniṣṭha-adhikārī* will not easily be able to understand the life of this great *uttama-bhāgavata* Vaiṣṇava. The higher things have been prohibited for us, but we should accept from his life whatever will be favourable for progress in the *madhyama-adhikārī* stage.

As long as we have not attained the mercy of Śrī Caitanya Mahāprabhu, Nityānanda Prabhu and Navadvīpa-dhāma, we will not be able to enter into Vraja. Therefore most of our previous *ācāryas* who were performing *bhajana* in Vṛndāvana left there and went to Navadvīpa to attain *prema*. Only after submerging themselves in the Gaṅgā of Mahāprabhu's *prema* in Navadvīpa did they return to Vṛndāvana to drown in the ocean of *kṛṣṇa-prema*. First they performed the *bhajana* of Gauracandra, and from that what did they attain? The *prema* of the amorous pastimes of Śrī Rādhā and Kṛṣṇa. Therefore, in the beginning Gaura-kiśora dāsa Bābājī Mahārāja performed *bhajana* in Vṛndāvana at Sūrya-kuṇḍa, Rādhā-kuṇḍa, Nandagrāma, Varṣāṇā and many other places; but in his heart came the feeling that, "The type of *prema* that I desire is not being attained here." He was performing *kīrtana* with great *prema*, calling out "Rādhā, Rādhā! Where have You gone? Protect my life because I will die without You! Rādhā, Rādhā!" Although he cried out with extreme *vipralambha-bhāva*, he felt that his yearning was not being fully satisfied, so he left Vṛndāvana and went to Navadvīpa. There, to avoid having to come in contact with worldly people, he lived in a latrine. He was such a *mahātmā* that he didn't even construct himself a hut.

Once, the aristocratic landholder of Kasima Bazar was organising a conference of all the prominent Vaiṣṇavas, and he approached Bābājī Mahārāja to request him to preside over this conference. He said, "Bābājī Mahārāja, I am organising a conference of Vaiṣṇavas, and everyone desires that you be the president of this assembly. Being merciful, please give *sukṛti* to us by accepting this entreaty, and I will take you there and bring you back in my own car."

Bābājī Mahārāja asked him, "For what purpose are you organising this conference? What is the necessity of doing it?"

The man replied, "It is for the preaching of *vaiṣṇava-dharma*, so people will hear talks describing Bhagavān and be inspired to take up *bhajana*."

Then Bābājī Mahārāja said, "Alright, then you do one thing: first you do *bhajana* and forget about others. Leave your home, wife and children, and come to me. I will furnish you with a pair of *kaupīnas* and then you do *bhajana*. First make your own life meaningful, and then worry about others. Otherwise your conference will only be for your own self-aggrandisement, and there will be no benefit in it for others anyway. First you should come to me and do *bhajana* for some time; then you should organise your conference." Hearing this strong answer from Bābājī Mahārāja, the man was rendered speechless and went away.

Another time, one man went to Bābājī Mahārāja and said, "Bābājī Mahārāja, please be merciful to me! Please be merciful to me!" Again and again he said it. Bābājī Mahārāja became a little annoyed and said, "You want mercy? Then here – take mercy!" and he handed the man a pair of *kaupīnas*. What is the purport of giving the man a pair of *kaupīnas*? When a *guru* gives *sannyāsa* to someone, what does he give him? A pair of *kaupīnas* and the *mantra*. Then that person will at once become renounced, leave all worldly attachments and fully apply his body, mind and words to the service of Kṛṣṇa. If the *guru* gives this to someone, what greater mercy could there be? "Here – take mercy!" Hearing this from Bābājī Mahārāja, that man became frightened, ran away and never returned.

On another occasion a young boy from a wealthy family ran away from home and came to Bābājī Mahārāja. He said to Bābājī Mahārāja, "I want to stay with you and just do *bhajana*." Bābājī Mahārāja did not reply, so the boy began staying with him. He would bring water for Bābājī Mahārāja and do other services for him also, and he began telling the people, "I am a disciple of Bābājī Mahārāja." But in reality Bābājī Mahārāja had no disciples other than Prabhupāda. This boy stayed with Bābājī Mahārāja for some time but didn't attain what he expected, so he thought, "I should return to material life." Many people go to live in a *maṭha*, stay for one or two months, and then return to material life, get married and become busy in household duties. Some men leave renounced life even after ten or twenty years, but only because they desired to attain the same things as worldly people: *kanaka* (wealth), *kāminī* (women) and *pratiṣṭhā* (prestige). They apparently leave their homes to engage in *bhajana*, but they are really only interested in material gain.

Feeling that he had attained nothing by staying with Bābājī Mahārāja, the boy left and after about two weeks returned to Bābājī Mahārāja with a beautiful young girl from a wealthy family whom he had married. He offered *praṇāma* to Bābājī Mahārāja and said, "Bābājī Mahārāja, I have entered the *saṁsāra*, the material world. Bhaktivinoda Ṭhākura has written in his *Gītāvalī*: *'kṛṣṇera saṁsāra kara chāḍi' anācāra* – we should give up our offences and perform *bhajana* as family men.' Therefore I have collected a *kṛṣṇa-dāsī*. Please be merciful to her and to me also so we can engage in *bhajana* and have a successful material life as well."

Bābājī Mahārāja replied, "You have done so well! I am so pleased! You have collected one *kṛṣṇa-dāsī*? Then you should do one thing: you should offer *pūjā* to this *kṛṣṇa-dāsī*. Every day you should cook an offering for her and offer her *praṇāma* and some flowers saying, 'You are a *kṛṣṇa-dāsī* and very dear to Śrī Kṛṣṇa.' But beware: don't try to enjoy her, otherwise everything will be destroyed for you and you will descend into hell! Beware – don't try to enjoy her!"

Hearing this, the boy was astonished and was rendered speechless. Frightened, he called his "*kṛṣṇa-dāsī*" and quickly left. Was deceiving Bābājī Mahārāja an easy thing? It was not possible to deceive him.

Bābājī Mahārāja vowed that he would never accept any disciples, but it was Prabhupāda's resolution that, "If I accept a *guru*, it will be him only." Prabhupāda wrote in his *Gauḍīya Patrikā*, "At that time I was very proud. I was thinking that there was no scholar equal to me, that there was no *tattva-jñānī* equal to me, no speaker equal to me and no philosopher equal to me. This *paramahaṁsa* Vaiṣṇava, Gaura-kiśora dāsa Bābājī Mahārāja, understood this; so he ignored my requests for initiation. Three or four times he told me that he would not accept disciples. He said, 'What? You are the son of Bhaktivinoda Ṭhākura! You took birth in such a high family that you are worshipful to me! You are such a big scholar, your appearance is so beautiful and you possess all good qualities; so what is the necessity of you becoming my disciple?' In this way he pulverised my pride. People said that he was illiterate, but he possessed all real knowledge and was a *jagad-guru*."

Three or four times Bābājī Mahārāja ignored him, but Prabhupāda had vowed that he would accept initiation only from Bābājī Mahārāja. In the end he was performing severe austerities to attain Bābājī Mahārāja as his *guru*, and seeing that his son's face was withered as if he would die, Bhaktivinoda Ṭhākura requested Bābājī Mahārāja, "Please be kind to him." After this, Bābājī Mahārāja finally accepted Prabhupāda as his only disciple.

Bhaktivinoda Ṭhākura's *āśrama* was situated on the banks of the Gaṅgā, and upon hearing "Hare Kṛṣṇa, Hare Kṛṣṇa, Kṛṣṇa Kṛṣṇa, Hare Hare, Hare Rāma, Hare Rāma, Rāma Rāma, Hare Hare" being chanted very loudly, Bhaktivinoda Ṭhākura would know that Bābājī Mahārāja was coming. He would chant so loudly that his voice could be heard across the Gaṅgā, and upon arrival at the *āśrama*, he would hear *Śrīmad-Bhāgavatam* and other *kṛṣṇa-kathā* from Bhaktivinoda Ṭhākura.

Bābājī Mahārāja didn't associate with other *bābājīs* very much. Generally he would only wear a *laṅgoṭī* and nothing more, but one day he begged a good quality *dhotī*, a *kurtā*, a walking stick and a nice turban from someone. Wearing these, he went to Bhaktivinoda Ṭhākura's *āśrama*, and upon seeing him, Bhaktivinoda Ṭhākura thought, "See how Bābājī Mahārāja's appearance has changed! He has taken the ordinary dress of a *gṛhastha*. He is wearing nice clothes now and is carrying a walking stick like a landlord. What has happened to him?"

Bābājī Mahārāja offered *praṇāma* and sat down, and Bhaktivinoda Ṭhākura asked him, "Bābājī Mahārāja, today I see that your appearance is of a different type. Why is this?"

Bābājī Mahārāja replied, "These days there are so many *bābājīs*, and many of them are such hooligans that if one even mentions their names it will be sinful. They are engaged in such misconduct that a *gṛhastha* is thousands of times superior to them. In the name of *parakīya-bhajana* they engage in mundane activities and they will all go to hell for it. When a *bābājī* obtains some *rasagullās* or any good quality foodstuff, he should just offer it to a cow. *Bābājīs* should not go to any festival, but people invite them and off they go to these festivals simply to enjoy a good meal. Feeding the dogs of the *dhāma* is more beneficial than feeding them. Therefore I think that I shouldn't remain a *bābājī*. I will wear the cloth of a *gṛhastha*, and then people will not look upon me as one of these *bābājīs*."

Bhaktivinoda Ṭhākura said, "You have spoken correctly." At that time the misconduct of these *bābājīs* was so widespread that people hated to even hear the good Vaiṣṇava name, so there was a necessity for a great personality who could preach the pure *prema-dharma* of Śrī Caitanya Mahāprabhu in the world. Then came such a great personality, Śrīla Bhaktisiddhānta Sarasvatī Prabhupāda. He preached *saṅkīrtana* in such a way that in no time the world opinion had changed, and scholars, gentlemen and everyone began to accept *vaiṣṇava-dharma*. If there had been no Gaura-kiśora dāsa Bābājī, then there would have been no Prabhupāda. And if there had been no Prabhupāda, then the pure *prema* of Mahāprabhu would not be preached all around the world as it is now. Therefore the original great personality was our father's father's father, our great grandfather, Gaura-kiśora dāsa Bābājī. Today with great pride we declare that he was the *guru* of our *parama-guru*, and it is our supreme good fortune that he came to this world.

According to our qualification we will follow the instructions for *bhajana* and renunciation that he gave, and those who sincerely follow them will be offering the real *puṣpāñjali* to his feet. Otherwise, if we don't offer this real *puṣpāñjali*, then we will be just like those people that he sent away. We should not desire to have material pleasures and at the same time beg for mercy as they did. For really achieving his mercy, we should offer this genuine *puṣpāñjali* to his feet, follow his instructions in a pure manner, and then we may be able to enter into real *bhajana*. He is never far away from us; he is with us at all times, and he will certainly bestow his plentiful mercy upon us. Calling out his name, our *gurujī* would cry and say, "He took all of my hardships away." Similarly he will remove all of our hardships so we will be able to perform *bhajana*, and to really engage in *bhajana* there must be no other desire whatsoever in our hearts. But if we leave *sādhu-saṅga*, all will be lost. Therefore, remaining in the association of devotees we will perform *bhajana* and always remember the ideal that Gaura-kiśora dāsa Bābājī Mahārāja showed in his life. Then our lives will be meaningful, and from our *bhajana* we will get the real benefit. So today we offer a prayer to his feet that he will always be merciful to all of us.

Chapter Six

The Disappearance Day of
Śrīla Raghunātha dāsa Gosvāmī

Śrīla Raghunātha dāsa Gosvāmī is an eternal associate of Caitanya Mahāprabhu and also of Kṛṣṇa, but in the pastimes of Mahāprabhu he showed the *sādhana-bhajana* for attaining the elevated devotional stages of *bhāva* and *prema*. If a *sādhaka* sincerely desires to engage in *bhajana* to achieve the direct association of Bhagavān without delay – perhaps in only one or two births – then he should engage in *bhajana* just as Raghunātha dāsa Gosvāmī did. But doing that type of *bhajana* is very, very difficult. How he left his home and family, how he engaged in very strict *bhajana*, how in his final days he went without eating and drinking and just cried day and night in divine separation – all of this would be very difficult for us. But for those who really desire *prema*, it is not so difficult.

This world is a reflection of the spiritual world; there is some similarity between them. If we see that this world is a place of instruction rather than a place for enjoyment, then we will be benefited. But only those who have taken sincere shelter at the feet of a *guru* will take such instruction; not everyone will be able to accept it. Dattātreya understood that this world is a place of instruction, and therefore he accepted twenty-four *gurus*. When we can fully understand the twenty-four *gurus* that have been mentioned, we will see that the entire world is our *guru*. Why has it been said that there are twenty-four *gurus*? Because there is nothing in all of existence from which some instruction cannot be taken. For an intelligent person, all the objects of the world will give some kind of instruction.

Someone may argue that the world is a prison-house which is full of unlimited misery.

tāvad rāgādayaḥ stenās
tāvat kārā-gṛhaṁ gṛham
tāvan moho 'ṅghri-nigado
yāvat kṛṣṇa na te janāḥ

Śrīmad-Bhāgavatam (10.14.36)

For those who are not devotees of Śrī Kṛṣṇa, the bewilderment of material attachment serves as the handcuffs and foot-shackles that bind them in the prison of *māyā*.

But the material world will not be a prison for those who are not infatuated with it. Here *rāga* means material attachment, which is like a thief and is the cause of our bondage. If this attachment is removed, then liberation will be attained. In this regard, Mahāprabhu told Raghunātha dāsa Gosvāmī:

sthira hañā ghare yāo, nā hao vātula
krame krame pāya loka bhava-sindhu-kūla

Śrī Caitanya-caritāmṛta (*Madhya-līlā* 16.237)

For now, return home and remain in household life. Don't behave irrationally. Eventually you will be able to cross the ocean of material existence.

If Bhagavān could be attained just by leaving home, then so many people would leave their homes because they couldn't get along with the other members of the household, or because of poverty or some other reason of this type. But would they attain the association of Bhagavān just by going to another place? Bhagavān is not attained merely by abandoning one's home and family. Especially if one abandons his home and family in an immature stage, it will be very detrimental to his welfare, and his condition may become even worse than that of an ordinary materialist. Bhagavān is attained only through abandoning material attachments and engaging in real *bhajana*. Therefore Mahāprabhu told Raghunātha dāsa Gosvāmī, "For now return home and be patient, and when the right time comes, you will automatically be able to leave everything." There is nothing in the material world that is inherently bad; it is only a question of proper or improper utilisation.

antare niṣṭhā kara, bāhye loka-vyavahāra
acirāt kṛṣṇa tomāya karibe uddhāra

Śrī Caitanya-caritāmṛta (*Madhya-līlā* 16.239)

Externally you should behave in an ordinary fashion with your family members, but internally you should have *niṣṭhā*. Then Kṛṣṇa will deliver you very soon.

But is having *niṣṭhā* an easy thing? What is *niṣṭhā*? Immovable, firm resolution. When there is firm confidence that whatever is said by *guru*, Vaiṣṇava and *śāstra* is correct, then that is called *śraddhā*. When this *śraddhā* becomes firm, it is called *niṣṭhā*. "I will give up my very life, but I will never leave the *bhajana* of Bhagavān. If I live at home or wherever, I will always engage in *bhajana*" – such resolution is called *niṣṭhā*. Honouring this instruction of Mahāprabhu, Raghunātha dāsa Gosvāmī returned home and began taking *harināma* and studying the scriptures, and at the same time attending to all of his worldly duties. Eventually his *niṣṭhā* increased more and more, and after attaining the mercy of Nityānanda Prabhu, he was able to leave his home permanently. He had tried to leave before and was unsuccessful, but Bhagavān could see the desire within him and therefore made the arrangement for him to leave.

When Bhagavān sees that there is sincere desire within us, He will make all arrangements for us to come to Him. Otherwise, if we try to make the necessary arrangements ourselves, we won't be able to enter into *bhajana* proper and we will eventually fall down. Therefore Bhagavān makes the arrangement for us, just as we see that He did for Gopa-kumāra in *Śrī Bṛhad-bhāgavatāmṛta*. In the form of *caitya-guru* in the heart He sees what is necessary and sends the *dīkṣā-guru* and the *śikṣā-guru* to us. Who gave Raghunātha dāsa Gosvāmī the company of Haridāsa Ṭhākura? Did Raghunātha dāsa Gosvāmī meet him of his own accord? The arrangement was made by Bhagavān. Haridāsa Ṭhākura used to visit the home of Raghunātha dāsa Gosvāmī – why? What was the necessity of his going there? Haridāsa Ṭhākura was a supreme renunciate; every day he would chant three *lākhas* of *harināma*. Therefore he could see the natural love and devotion for Bhagavān that the young boy Raghunātha dāsa possessed, so he would go to his home and teach him how to take *harināma*. Of course, Raghunātha dāsa had the previous *saṁskāra* of a perfected soul, but here we can see how Bhagavān makes the arrangement for a *sādhaka* to acquire the association of a great personality. And He also sent Yadunandana Ācārya, a disciple of Advaita Ācārya, to become Raghunātha dāsa's *dīkṣā-guru*.

sthāne sthitāḥ śruti-gatāṁ tanu-vāṅ-manobhir
ye prāyaśo 'jita jito 'py asi tais tri-lokyām

Śrīmad-Bhāgavatam (10.14.3)

Even while remaining within their respective social positions, fortunate souls get the opportunity to hear *hari-kathā* from great personalities, and becoming inspired to dedicate their body, mind and words, they conquer He who is otherwise unconquerable by anyone within the three worlds.

Bhagavān made this arrangement for Raghunātha dāsa, and within a short time intense eagerness arose within his heart and he thought, "How will I attain the direct association of Bhagavān? What kind of *sādhana-bhajana* should I perform?" Then he went to Pānihāṭi where he received the *darśana* of Nityānanda Prabhu. On the order of Nityānanda Prabhu, Raghunātha dāsa arranged a big festival; and by the power of his meditation Nityānanda Prabhu, called Mahāprabhu Himself to attend it. When Raghunātha dāsa received the *darśana* of the two brothers taking *prasāda* together, this increased his desire even more. Then Nityānanda Prabhu placed his lotus feet on Raghunātha dāsa's head and said, "Now all your obstructions will disappear." So by the mercy of Nityānanda Prabhu he was able to leave his home and travel to Purī where he attained the shelter of Mahāprabhu's feet. This time Mahāprabhu gave him another type of instruction:

'mane' nija-siddha-deha kariyā bhāvana
rātri-dine kare vraje kṛṣṇera sevana

Śrī Caitanya-caritāmṛta (*Madhya-līlā* 22.157)

"Internally a perfected soul thinks day and night of serving Kṛṣṇa in Vṛndāvana, and Svarūpa Dāmodara will teach you this very special activity." Mahāprabhu didn't personally give Raghunātha dāsa so much instruction, but He handed him over to one of His eternal associates from whom he received all instruction. And what did Svarūpa Dāmodara teach him? To perform the high standard of *bhajana* that he himself did.

Svarūpa Dāmodara would compose *ślokas* describing the ontological position of Mahāprabhu, and he also kept a diary describing the daily pastimes of Mahāprabhu. For instance, he wrote that one night, when the waves of *bhāva* were powerfully flowing through Mahāprabhu's heart, He somehow managed to pass through three bolted doors. He mistook the ocean for the Kālindī, and thinking the waves to be due to the sporting of Kṛṣṇa with the *gopīs*, He jumped in. Floating farther and farther away, He came into the net of a fisherman at Ārkatīrtha. When the fisherman brought the devotees to Mahāprabhu, they saw that all of His joints were dislocated, His limbs were all elongated and He was rolled up into a round shape. This is a symptom of *mahābhāva*. This will not happen in the stages of *prema*, *sneha*, *māna*, *praṇaya*, *rāga* or even *anurāga*. Sometimes this will not even happen in *mahābhāva*, but only in the higher stages of *ruḍha*, *adhiruḍha*, *madana* and *citra-jalpa*. But this may not even come within *citra-jalpa*, which is where Śrīmatī Rādhikā, in the madness of divine separation, was speaking to a bee about Kṛṣṇa. We don't find any description of Her ever displaying the symptoms that Mahāprabhu did here.

Svarūpa Dāmodara recorded these pastimes in his diary and revealed them all to Raghunātha dāsa Gosvāmī. Then later Raghunātha dāsa revealed them to Kṛṣṇadāsa Kavirāja Gosvāmī. Murāri Gupta, who was an incarnation of Hanumān, also kept a diary. But since his feelings were for *dāsya-rasa*, he found other pastimes of Mahāprabhu to be more tasteful, and therefore he described them. Svarūpa Dāmodara was Lalitā herself, so in his poetry he described the *mahābhāva* and higher conditions of Mahāprabhu. Just see what an excellent arrangement Mahāprabhu made for Raghunātha dāsa Gosvāmī: He handed him over to Svarūpa Dāmodara who taught him all of these things. If we ever receive such a good opportunity, then we should understand that it was arranged by Bhagavān Himself. For a *sādhaka* who is especially sincere, He will make such an arrangement, but one who is not so eager will not receive such good fortune.

At first Mahāprabhu instructed Raghunātha dāsa to remain at home, and this instruction was in relation to *vaidhī-bhakti*. The instruction that He gave later – that a perfected soul deeply remembers Kṛṣṇa day and night – was on the *rāgānugā* level, and Raghunātha dāsa harmonised both of these in his life. Śrīla Bhaktisiddhānta Sarasvatī Prabhupāda also gave instructions related to *vaidhī-bhakti*, such as instructions for *arcana*, while at the same time drawing forth the sentiments of *rāgānugā* from the poetry of *Śrīmad-Bhāgavatam*. He combined them in his preaching in this world. Regardless if people were qualified or unqualified, Prabhupāda accepted everyone. Previously there was a prohibition that only those who were especially qualified could leave their homes and families and come to engage in *bhajana*; but everyone received a good opportunity from Prabhupāda. He created a school in which even those who were unqualified could come and learn, and gradually progress upwards. Otherwise we would not have the qualification to come in this line, but he opened the door for everyone.

These days society has become somewhat degraded. Young boys no longer honour the conventions of society or accept the guidance of their parents as they did previously. They sometimes fall into bad company and become thieves and dacoits, and then it becomes almost impossible for them to be rectified and find the correct path. But Prabhupāda made schools and centres in Māyāpura and all over India in which these boys could come. Perhaps they only had a little taste for spiritual life, but he saw their potential to eventually have complete taste. They learned something there and made substantial progress in the direction of pure *bhajana*, sometimes even up to the point of becoming *brahmacārīs*. Those who desired to do so could after some time return to their homes, marry and perform *bhajana* there; Prabhupāda didn't impose any restriction on that. In this way Mahāprabhu's mission was spread throughout India.

As long as Mahāprabhu remained within this world, Raghunātha dāsa Gosvāmī stayed near Him, and when He disappeared, Raghunātha dāsa became so disturbed that he at once gave up eating. Then in a short time Svarūpa Dāmodara, Rāya Rāmānanda and Gadādhara Paṇḍita all left this world. Because everything then appeared void in Purī, all the remaining devotees left there. The very things there that had previously been so dear to Raghunātha dāsa now pained him like thorns. His condition was like that of the residents of Vraja after Kṛṣṇa had departed for Mathurā. When Kṛṣṇa was in Vṛndāvana, the *sakhās* and *sakhīs* loved Nanda-bhavana very dearly. The *gopīs* loved the Yamunā's Gopī-ghāṭa so much because there they would meet Kṛṣṇa. They loved Govardhana so much because there were so many beautiful gardens and *kuñjas* there where they would make flower garlands for Kṛṣṇa. Blissfully they would go to these places, but when Kṛṣṇa departed for Mathurā, Nanda-bhavana appeared empty and lifeless. The *gopīs'* remembrance of Kṛṣṇa became so intense that they no longer desired to go there, and everywhere they cast their vision drowned them in *vipralambha-rasa*. Food was no longer prepared there, the utensils were just lying around and there were cobwebs everywhere. Who would they prepare food for? Mother Yaśodā had become almost blind in separation. In an attempt to forget Kṛṣṇa, Nanda Bābā left there, but there was no place in Vraja that would allow forgetfulness of Kṛṣṇa. Everything just brought more remembrance of Him.

After Mahāprabhu left this world, the devotees in Purī were in exactly the same condition. For Raghunātha dāsa, going to the Gambhīrā was like entering a fire, and day and night he only cried and cried. This is real *bhajana*, and until one's *bhajana* is of this standard, it is only *ābhāsa*, or the shadow of real *bhajana*. Unless one has experienced such intense feelings of separation from Kṛṣṇa, *guru* and the Vaiṣṇavas, they have not entered into real *bhajana*. Mahāprabhu Himself showed the way: He was always lamenting, "Where can I find Vrajendra-nandana? Where has He gone?" Day and night He was crying, feeling the full impact of divine separation.

Sometimes we also cry, but for what reason? Because we have just received some indication that our material attachments and enjoyment may be taken away from us. Inside we should be feeling intense separation from Mahāprabhu, from Śrī Rādhā and Kṛṣṇa, and if not directly from Them, then from our own *guru*. But we have no experience of these feelings of the upper world, and instead we only desire material happiness. But really we belong exclusively to Them, and with that understanding we should approach this line of devotion. Therefore, first there should be deep attachment for *bhajana*, and then for *bhajanīya*, those whom we are worshipping. In our conditioned state we are not as much concerned about chanting our daily prescribed number of rounds as we are about things like, "What will I eat? Where will I live?" But how did Raghunātha dāsa Gosvāmī perform *bhajana*? His only anxiety was: "How will I do *bhajana*? How can I make sure that this life is not wasted, and how will I attain Bhagavān in this very life?"

For those of us aspiring for *rāgānuga-bhakti*, the life of Raghunātha dāsa Gosvāmī is very instructive, and if we can assimilate into our lives even one iota of his eagerness for *bhajana*, we will surely become successful. Regardless of whether we are renunciates or householders, we should have some of the eagerness for *bhajana* that he did. If we have that eagerness, all of our endeavours will automatically become crowned with success.

Chapter Seven

Advaita Saptamī

Advaita Saptamī is the day that Advaita Ācārya appeared in this world. Advaita Ācārya, the cause of the material world, comes first; after that Nityānanda Prabhu comes on the day of *trayodaśī*; and then Śrī Caitanya Mahāprabhu Himself comes on *pūrṇimā*, descending into this world with the effulgence of *rādhā-bhāva*. In this way the pastimes of Mahāprabhu begin.

vande taṁ śrīmad-advaitā-
cāryam adbhuta-ceṣṭitam
yasya prasādād ajño 'pi
tat-svarūpam nirūpayet

Śrī Caitanya-caritāmṛta (*Ādi-līlā* 6.1)

I pray to Advaita Ācārya, who performs especially wonderful pastimes, that by his mercy I may be able to describe this difficult *tattva* easily. What are these wonderful pastimes? Seeing Nityānanda Prabhu, Advaita Prabhu began complaining: "Where has this *avadhūta* come from? Today he has come to our home and thrown *prasāda* in all directions! He has no knowledge of what class he belongs to; actually he has no class at all! We are *brāhmaṇas*, we are the best of society, and he has dropped *prasāda* on the bodies of everyone here!"

Then Nityānanda Prabhu said, "Hey, *aparādhī*! You are committing an offence to *mahā-prasāda*. You consider it to be mere food, and that it is merely being thrown around? You can't see that it bestows good fortune, and that whoever's body is touched by this *prasāda* at once crosses over *māyā*."

In this way, there was generally some quarrelling between them. When they would go for bathing, then certainly there would be quarrelling. At that time Nityānanda Prabhu was very young. Mahāprabhu was the youngest, next came Nityānanda, and the oldest of all was Advaita Ācārya, whose thoughts are sometimes very difficult to understand. He sent a mysterious sonnet to Mahāprabhu.

bāulake kahiha, – loka ha-ila bāula
bāulake kahiha, – hāṭe nā vikāya cāula

bāulake kahiha, – kāye nāhika āula
bāulake kahiha, – ihā kahiyāche bāula

Śrī Caitanya-caritāmṛta (*Antya-līlā* 19.20–1)

One madman is sending a message to another madman. There is no longer necessity for rice in the marketplace, so it is time for the shop to be closed.

No one could understand this sonnet. Upon reading it, Mahāprabhu was a little indifferent. Only Svarūpa Dāmodara could understand a little of Advaita Ācārya's mood; no one else could understand. And he said that one madman – Advaita Ācārya, who is mad with *kṛṣṇa-prema* – is sending a message to another madman – Śrī Caitanya Mahāprabhu, the one who made the world mad with *kṛṣṇa-prema*, the original madness. "There is no longer necessity for rice" means that *prema* has been given to everyone, and now the task is completed. "Therefore the shop should be closed" means "Your pastimes in the material world should now come to a close." But no one understood this; only Svarūpa Dāmodara could know something of its meaning. In this way Advaita Ācārya's pastimes were mysterious and wonderful.

Although the gist of *Bhagavad-gītā* advocates *bhakti*, at the time of Advaita Prabhu's appearance no one was explaining it in that way. The message of the *Gītā* is full of devotion – *viśate tad anantaram* (*Bhagavad-gītā* (18.55)): "Ultimately he enters into Me." *Advaitavādīs* interpret this to mean that Bhagavān and the *jīva* merge in Brahman and become one. They say that by chanting "*ahaṁ brahmāsmi*" and practising meditation, the apparent individuality of the souls merge in the end, and that the material world is false. Advaita Ācārya first of all gave the explanation of *bhakti* from these verses: *satataṁ kīrtayanto mām* (*Bhagavad-gītā* (9.14)); *ananyāś cintayanto māṁ, ye janāḥ paryupāsate* (9.22); and *bhakti labhate parām* (18.54) – in the end, we will attain *bhakti*. By the medium of the precepts described in these verses, then *viśate tad anantaram* – we enter into *bhakti*. Not that we meet Bhagavān in Brahman, entering into undifferentiated light. *Viśate* means that we enter into His *dhāma* and attain His service, but some people were trying to change the meaning.

After some time, Advaita Ācārya went to Śāntipura and also started explaining the meaning of *viśate tad anantaram* as "*ahaṁ brahmāsmi*: all souls will merge in Brahman." Hearing of this, Mahāprabhu went there and pulled his beard and beat him until Sītā-devī, Advaita Ācārya's wife, came and protected him. This is also wonderful because having been beaten, Śrī Advaita became very pleased and started dancing. Previously, Mahāprabhu was offering *praṇāma* to him and offering him respect befitting one's *guru* because Advaita Prabhu was a disciple of Mādhavendra Purī. Mahāprabhu was thinking, "He is a disciple of My *parama-guru*, so it is My duty to offer *praṇāma* and *sevā* to him. He is worshipful to Me, and therefore I should serve and worship him."

For ridding Himself of this service, Advaita Ācārya gave the impersonalist *nirviśesavāda* explanation of *Bhagavad-gītā*. When Mahāprabhu became angry and started beating him, Advaita Ācārya said, "Today my life has become successful. I wanted You to accept service from me, because You are senior to me. Who can possibly be senior to You?" Mahāprabhu then became shy.

Another time, Mahāprabhu said to His mother Śacī-devī, "I will not show love to you anymore because you have disrespected a devotee. You have committed *vaiṣṇava-aparādha*. You told Advaita Prabhu that, 'Your name Advaita (meaning non-dual) is not suitable; rather your name should be Dvaita (dual). You are not *advaita*, you are *dvaita*.' What you said was that Advaita Ācārya brings 'duality', separation in relationships – that he separates a mother from her son, a father from his son, a brother from his brother. Advaita Ācārya explains the path of devotion, thereby breaking the chains that bind one to the material world. A mother has natural affection for her offspring, but if Advaita Prabhu is able to increase someone's spontaneous attraction towards Kṛṣṇa, then what could be greater than that? If someone is giving the instruction that the *jīva* has forgotten Bhagavān for millions of births, and then establishes *sambandha* (knowledge of our true relationship with Bhagavān) and *sādhya* (the final attainment), and gives instruction for *bhajana* that cuts the chains that bind us to the material world, what could be greater than that?"

Śacī-devī replied, "He separated me from my beloved Viśvarūpa. He gave such instruction that it separated me from Viśvarūpa, who left home and became a *sannyāsī*. Therefore 'Advaita' means that person whom having met once, one will not desire anything within this world. So his name should be 'Dvaita' instead."

Mahāprabhu said, "Since you spoke to a devotee in this way, none of us will show you love anymore."

As she stood there, everyone told her that because she had committed an offence at the feet of Advaita Ācārya, they could not show any love to her. Then Śacī-devī went to beg forgiveness from Advaita Ācārya, but instead he fell at her feet and said, "You are the mother of the entire world. It is not possible for you to commit any offence. But alright, if someone says that there has been some offence, then I say it is hereby forgiven." Then Śacī-devī returned to Mahāprabhu and everything was set right. Many wonderful pastimes like this were performed by Śrī Advaita Prabhu.

Advaita Ācārya was also instrumental in bringing Śrī Caitanya Mahāprabhu to this world. At the end of Dvāpara-yuga, upon completing His pastimes in this world and returning to Goloka Vṛndāvana, Śrī Kṛṣṇacandra thought, "I have three desires that have not yet been fulfilled. Understanding the glories of Rādhikā's love, discovering the sweetness that She finds within Me, and tasting that sweetness – without assuming the sentiment of Rādhikā Herself and the effulgence of Her form, it will not be possible to experience these three things. I have tasted *sakhya-rasa*, *vātsalya-rasa* and *mādhurya-rasa*, but as yet I have been unable to experience what Her happiness is upon seeing Me, and what is the nature of Her *prema* for Me. In order to experience this, I must again go to the material world."

At that time it was necessary for the *yuga-dharma* to be given. The age of Kali, which lasts for 432,000 years, had come. Ordinarily, at the end of each *yuga* an incarnation of Bhagavān comes, just as at the end of Tretā-yuga, Rāmacandra came, and at the end of Dvāpara-yuga, Kṛṣṇa came. Such a *yuga-avatāra* comes when the disorder in the material world has reached its highest limit.

dharma-saṁsthāpanārthāya
sambhavāmi yuge yuge

Bhagavad-gītā (4.8)

In order to re-establish the principles of religion, I appear millennium after millennium.

Bhagavān thinks, "Just see how much sinful activity is increasing and how the chaos is escalating due to the demons. When should I descend?"

So there are actually four reasons for Mahāprabhu's descent. Two are primary, and two are secondary. The most primary reason is for tasting the *prema* of Rādhikā, and the second reason is:

anarpita-carīṁ cirāt karuṇayāvatīrṇaḥ kalau
samarpayitum unnatojjvala-rasāṁ sva-bhakti-śriyam

Śrī Caitanya-caritāmṛta (*Ādi-līlā* 1.4)

> By His causeless mercy He appears in the age of Kali to bestow what no incarnation has ever offered before: *unnata ujjvala-rasa* – the most sublime amorous mellow in His own service.

Mahāprabhu wanted to give a specific wealth of *prema* to the *jīvas* that had never been bestowed by any previous incarnations: *unnata-ujjvala-rasa* – the *parakīya-bhāva* of the *gopīs*. There are two kinds of *unnata-ujjvala-parakīya-rasa*. One kind, the sentiment of Rādhikā, is not "giveable". But the other, the sentiment of the *nitya-sakhīs* and the *prāṇa-sakhīs* who serve Rādhā, and who, following Her, also serve Kṛṣṇa – that *unnata-ujjvala-rasa* can be given. Therefore to bestow the highest *prema* upon all *jīvas* and to taste the *prema* of Rādhikā, Kṛṣṇa comes.

His third reason for coming is to preach the *yuga-dharma*, *nāma-saṅkīrtana*; and the fourth reason is:

yadā yadā hi dharmasya
glānir bhavati bhārata
abhyutthānam adharmasya
tadātmānaṁ sṛjāmy aham

Bhagavad-gītā (4.7)

> Whenever and wherever there is a decline in religious practice, O descendent of Bharata, and a predominant rise of irreligion – at that time I descend.

These are the four reasons.

Kṛṣṇa was thinking, "When should I go? To establish the *yuga-dharma*, descending at the end of the *yuga* is alright, but if instead I preach *nāma-saṅkīrtana* at the beginning of the *yuga*, the degrading influence of the *yuga* will have a lesser effect on the *jīvas*. When should I give the sentiment of the *gopīs*, and when should I taste the love of Rādhikā?" He was considering all of these things.

Meanwhile Advaita Ācārya saw that *bhakti* was gradually disappearing from the world, and he thought, "Now is the appropriate time for Kṛṣṇa's incarnation. If He doesn't come now, what will happen later?" At the same time, he was also thinking this in the form of Kāraṇodakaśāyī Viṣṇu. He was pondering in that place where *sattva*, *rajas* and *tamas* are all in the same position. There are two causes of the world: one is *upādāna*, the ingredient cause, and the other is *nimitta*, the efficient cause. Mahā-Viṣṇu himself is the *nimitta* cause, and his part, Advaita Ācārya, is the *upādāna* cause.

Suppose I were to point to someone and say, "This man is a hooligan, thief and liar. Grab him and throw him outside; he should never be allowed in here again." Now you may not know him, but by my saying this, you throw him out. So who is the cause of him being thrown out? By my order you grabbed this man and ejected him, so you are the *upādāna* cause, and I am the *nimitta* cause. But who is the real cause of the man being ejected? By his own misbehaviour, the man himself is the cause; and this is exactly the situation regarding the creation of the material world.

Kāraṇodakaśāyī Viṣṇu assumes two forms to create the material world: as the efficient cause and the ingredient cause. When the two of them come together, countless *brahmāṇḍas* are generated. But if Bhagavān did not inject His desire, then what? In any activity, there is first the desire for it to take place. Therefore the desire of Mahā-Viṣṇu is the primary cause, and dependent on His desire is the desire of Advaita Ācārya, which is the secondary cause. In this way Kāraṇodakaśāyī Viṣṇu performs the activity of creating the world, and His incarnation is Advaita Ācārya.

advaita-ācārya gosāñi sākṣāt īśvara
yāṅhāra mahimā nahe jīvera gocara

Śrī Caitanya-caritāmṛta (*Ādi-līlā* 6.6)

Śrī Advaita Ācārya is directly the Īśvara Himself. His glories cannot be comprehended by ordinary living beings.

From *mahat-tattva*, false ego arises. From false ego comes sound, touch, form, taste and smell. Next come the eleven senses, and next are the five material elements. That makes twenty-two, and with the intelligence and mind it makes twenty-four. Then adding *prakṛti*, *puruṣa*, *ātmā* and Paramātmā makes twenty-eight aspects of *tattva* altogether. Leaving aside Bhagavān and *jīvātmā*, only the remainder are accepted by the *sāṅkhya* and the *nyāya* schools of thought.

ye puruṣa sṛṣṭi-sthiti karena māyāya
ananta brahmāṇḍa sṛṣṭi karena līlāya
icchāya ananta mūrti karena prakāśa
eka eka mūrte karena brahmāṇḍe praveśa
se puruṣera aṁśa – advaita, nāhi kichu bheda
śarīra-viśeṣa tāṅra – nāhika viccheda
sahāya karena tāṅra la-iyā 'pradhāna'
koṭi brahmāṇḍa karena icchāya nirmāṇa

Śrī Caitanya-caritāmṛta (*Ādi-līlā* 6.8–11)

Mahā-Viṣṇu performs the function of creation of all the material universes, and Advaita Ācārya is directly an incarnation of him. Creating and maintaining these countless universes by his external energy is his pastime, and by his own will he expands into countless forms and enters into each and every universe. Advaita Ācārya is a non-different part and parcel of Mahā-Viṣṇu, or in other words, another form of him.

Some say that nature enacts the process of creation by itself, and they give this example: "A cow eats grass, and automatically milk is produced. What is the necessity of anyone else in this process? In this way nature does everything by itself."

To refute this, an innocent, less-educated Vaiṣṇava said, "The cow eats grass and then gives milk, so why then doesn't the bull eat grass and also give milk? Does he need to eat more grass?"

The *paṇḍita* of the *sāṅkhya* school had to think for a moment. Then he said, concerning the *upādāna* cause, "To make a house, all elements such as bricks are necessary."

Then the Vaiṣṇava said, "So if by bricks or cement a house will be made, then here we will place one thousand kilos of cement, ten thousand bricks, an entire lake of water, and wood and marble also. Will that make a house? By the *upādāna* only it will not happen because it needs the *nimitta* cause. There may be a pen and paper, but by themselves will they write? Therefore, by the material nature alone creation will not take place as long as the desire of Bhagavān is not there."

No action can take place by itself in the material world, so therefore this *prakṛtivāda* philosophy is erroneous. *Prakṛti* means matter, *puruṣa* is conscious, and when both come together there is creation. In *prakṛti* there is no action, no innate desire – it is inert matter. But when it is activated by the *puruṣa*, then automatically the task is accomplished. The communists say, "What is the need of God in this? Nature creates by itself," but there is no one in the world who can create by himself.

A lame man and a blind man were going somewhere together and the lame man said, "Take me on your shoulders. Seeing with my eyes, I will tell you to go right, left or straight on the path, and with your legs we will go there. Otherwise you will not be able to go there, and neither will I." Working together, they reached their desired destination. In this example the lame man is conscious, and the blind man is also conscious, and both being conscious, the work was done. But in creation only Bhagavān is conscious, and nature is not. Without at least one conscious being no work in the world can be done. These issues may seem a little dry, but they are very important and tasteful points related to *bhakti*, and Vaiṣṇavas should make an effort to understand them.

In all of this *tattva*, the root cause of the material world is Kṛṣṇa because originally He injects His desire. He becomes two kinds of Saṅkarṣaṇa: the root Saṅkarṣaṇa and Mahā-Saṅkarṣaṇa. From Mahā-Saṅkarṣaṇa He becomes Kāraṇodakaśāyī Viṣṇu, and subsequently He becomes Advaita Ācārya and the *upādāna* cause. Some people say that the *upādāna* cause is separate from Bhagavān, that the *upādāna* cause of the material world is not Bhagavān. They say that He may be the *nimitta* cause, but He cannot be the *upādāna* cause. But besides Kṛṣṇa there is nothing, so from where has the material world come? From where has the *mahat-tattva* come? It has also come from the desire of Kṛṣṇa. There is nothing in all of existence that is separate from Him. Kāraṇodakaśāyī manifests the creation, and the *mahat-tattva*, nature herself, is thus non-different from Him. To correct the souls that have forgotten Bhagavān, *prakṛti* is manifest by His desire and gives the *jīva* an external form. The *jīva* may consider his placement in that condition of life to be an opportunity for great happiness, but actually it is punishment. Just like when a crazy man dances around naked – people will beat him, and without eating or drinking he wanders around. He says, "I am the king" or "I am the prime minister" and he thinks himself to be happy. Our condition is exactly like that. We may consider ourselves happy, but in reality we are not in a happy condition at all.

Thus Advaita Ācārya was thinking, "The world has become atheistic. One after another, people are forgetting Bhagavān, and for me to rectify them alone is not possible. To bring devotion to the non-devotees will be very, very difficult work. Without the *śakti* of Kṛṣṇa Himself, it simply cannot be done."

Besides devotees, there are so many people in the world who are preaching, but they are all preaching *māyā*. They are preaching twisted philosophies, and seeing this, Śrī Advaita thought, "They have no relation with Bhagavān and they do not preach *bhakti*. Even when they do preach from *Śrīmad-Bhāgavatam* and *Bhagavad-gītā*, they express only the desires of their minds. They are indifferent to *sanātana-dharma* and pure devotion, and all of them – especially the *māyāvādīs* – will only hear what they want to hear. Defeating Rāvaṇa was not a very difficult thing, and killing Kaṁsa was also not a difficult thing. These actions could have been done by a Viṣṇu incarnation, but changing the thinking of these *māyāvādīs* is very difficult. Only if Kṛṣṇa Himself comes into this world will it be possible."

Since Advaita Prabhu was at least sixty years old when Mahāprabhu appeared, he was the oldest of all of Mahāprabhu's associates. Nityānanda Prabhu was approximately five years older than Mahāprabhu. Mahāprabhu's plan was that He would first arrange for His devotees to appear in this world, and then He would descend Himself. Advaita Ācārya appeared first, and seeing the condition of the world, he thought, "How will I call Kṛṣṇa? There are so many types of worship of Kṛṣṇa, but amongst all of these, the glories of *tulasī* are the greatest. Kṛṣṇa will be so pleased with anyone who offers Him a *tulasī* leaf and Ganges water that it will overpower Him." Thus he took a *tulasī* bud – two soft leaves with a *mañjarī* in the middle – and, with great *prema* and tears flowing from his eyes, worshipped Kṛṣṇa beside the Ganges.

Kṛṣṇa was originally thinking, "When will I descend? Maybe in ten or twenty thousand years, or maybe even after one hundred thousand years." But upon hearing Advaita Ācārya's prayer, He came at once. Therefore Advaita Ācārya is another primary reason for the descent of Mahāprabhu.

At birth, Śrī Advaita was given the name Kamalākṣa because his eyes were as beautiful as lotus petals. He appeared at Srihatta in East Bengal. Staying sometimes in Navadvīpa and sometimes in Śāntipura, he began preaching *bhakti*. He was there in Navadvīpa when Mahāprabhu took birth. Viśvarūpa attended Advaita Prabhu's school. One day

Mother Śacī told Nimāi to go and call His brother; so when He arrived at the school, Nimāi glanced in the direction of Advaita Ācārya and said, "What do you see? You called Me here and you don't recognise Me? When the proper time comes, you will certainly recognise Me."

There are unlimited incarnations of Viṣṇu and they are all non-different from Kṛṣṇa, but their activities and pastimes are different. Therefore, because Advaita Ācārya is non-different from Hari, he is *advaita*, and because he manifested *bhakti* in all directions, he is known as *ācārya*. How did he preach *bhakti*? If anyone was born in a *śūdra* family, a Muslim family or any family, and performed *bhagavad-bhajana*, Advaita Prabhu considered him better than a *brāhmaṇa* who didn't engage in *bhajana*. If there is someone who has taken birth in a high *brāhmaṇa* family, is an eminent scholar, of good conduct, speaks the truth and never lies, but does not engage in *bhagavad-bhajana*, then he is inferior to one who has taken birth in a *śūdra* family or in a family of cremation-ground workers, if that person just cries out "Kṛṣṇa! Kṛṣṇa!" and does no other spiritual activity whatsoever. That *śūdra* is superior to a *caturvedī-brāhmaṇa*: Advaita Ācārya proved this point and preached it.

Haridāsa Ṭhākura was born in a Muslim family. At the *śrāddha* ceremony for Advaita Ācārya's father, the highest seat and *prasāda* were to be offered first to the most elevated person. Advaita Ācārya was performing the ceremony when the moon was in the appropriate place in the month of Āśvina. All the high-class *brāhmaṇas* were there – Bhaṭṭācārya, Trivedī, Caturvedī, Upādhyāya – and all of them were great scholars. After washing their feet, Advaita Ācārya showed them to their respective seats. In front was an elevated seat, and Advaita Prabhu was standing and thinking, "Who will I seat here?"

All of the scholars were thinking, "I know so many scriptures; certainly I will be offered that seat." Silently they were all aspiring for it. Advaita Ācārya then went outside the house and saw Haridāsa Thākura, wearing a *laṅgoṭī* and sitting at the door. Haridāsa was thinking, "The *brāhmaṇas* will take their meal here, so Advaita Ācārya will certainly give us a little of their *prasāda.*" He had so much humility that he was thinking that if he went inside, the house would be contaminated. At once Advaita Ācārya embraced him, and Haridāsa Ṭhākura said, "Oh, you are a *brāhmaṇa* and I am a Muslim! Having touched me, you must now go and bathe." But grabbing him and taking him inside, Advaita Ācārya sat him on the elevated seat, at which time there was a great outcry in all directions. The *brāhmaṇas* said, "By bringing a Muslim in here, you have contaminated this place and insulted us! We will not eat here!" Taking their water pots, they all stood up and left. They were abusing Advaita Ācārya, saying, "You are opposed to the principles of *dharma*!"

But Advaita Ācārya said, "Today my birth has become successful, and today my father has attained Vaikuṇṭha. By giving respect to one Vaiṣṇava, today millions of my ancestors have crossed over *māyā*. If Haridāsa Ṭhākura will eat here, then that is greater than feeding millions of *brāhmaṇas.*"

Haridāsa Ṭhākura was crying, thinking, "Because of me, all these *brāhmaṇas* have been insulted and are not eating."

But Advaita Ācārya said, "Haridāsa, today you will certainly take *prasāda* here. That will be our great good fortune." Then he said to the *brāhmaṇas*, "He will stay, and none of you will get *prasāda*. Actually, you should all leave here quickly, because just seeing your faces is a great sin. Haridāsa has great regard for *mahā-prasāda*, and therefore he is included within the Vaiṣṇava class. Anyone who doesn't accept this is an atheist, and one who judges a Vaiṣṇava by his birth is an atheist. You can all go away from here and then your offences will leave with you. You are offending Haridāsa, and offending me as well."

All the scholars left the house, but outside, as they were going, they began speaking amongst themselves. "Advaita Ācārya is no ordinary personality. He is a great scholar, he knows all of the scriptures and he is an exalted preacher of *bhakti*." They continued deliberating, and after fully reconsidering, they returned, fell at Advaita Prabhu's feet and begged forgiveness.

Advaita Ācārya had many sons, of which one was named Acyutānanda, but because some of his other sons didn't engage in *bhajana*, he didn't consider them his sons at all and he renounced them. Only those sons who performed *bhajana* of Bhagavān did he make his successors. Especially because of one incident in Jagannātha Purī, Acyutānanda was made his successor. The Ratha-yātrā was going on, and at that time Acyutānanda was just a small boy. Some Vaiṣṇavas came and asked Advaita Ācārya, "What is the name of Śrī Caitanya Mahāprabhu's *guru*?" He replied, "Keśava Bhāratī."

At that time, Acyutānanda was sitting in his father's lap, and upon hearing this he began shivering with anger. He was just a small boy! Nevertheless, he got up from his father's lap and started to walk away, saying, "You cannot be my father if you have such an idea. Śrī Caitanya Mahāprabhu is the *guru* of the entire world! Who can possibly be His *guru*?"

Tears came to the eyes of Advaita Ācārya, and he said, "You will really be known as my son. What you have said is correct: Mahāprabhu is the *guru* of the entire world, but for His pastimes in human form He must set the example for others. Otherwise what would happen? How would the people of this world know that it is necessary to accept a *guru*?"

In this way Advaita Ācārya did many wonderful things. He was an assistant to all of the pastimes of Śrī Caitanya Mahāprabhu. Therefore today we will offer a special prayer to the feet of Advaita Ācārya that he may be merciful upon us so that we can make steady progress in *bhakti* and ultimately attain the direct service of Śrī Gauracandra.

Chapter Eight

Nityānanda Trayodaśī

Once there was a barber who was going here and there giving out invitations. In previous times barbers performed this task for families. If there was to be a marriage or a festival, he would go and distribute the invitations to everyone, and for doing this he would earn a little extra money. But he would not go anywhere without his instruments such as a razor, scissors and a comb.

Starting on his way, this barber entered a jungle where he saw a lion resting on the path. The lion did not attack him, but instead was merely lifting up its paw and licking it. At first the barber was frightened, but then he thought, "It seems that there is something stuck in his foot, and that is why he is not attacking." So the barber went a little nearer and saw that a very large thorn was stuck in very deeply, and due to this the lion was suffering greatly. Therefore, with the help of his instruments, the barber manipulated the thorn a little and carefully removed it. Some blood had been coming from the wound, so he also applied some antiseptic, wrapped the lion's paw in some medicinal leaves, and then left.

Three or four years went by. Then one day that same barber was mistakenly arrested for some very serious crime such as murder. His case was brought before the king, who said, "Several days ago in the jungle we captured a lion.

Throw the criminal into the lion's compartment. The lion will eat him – finished. For him there can be no other punishment. Throw him in!"

The barber was thrown into the lion's cage, and at once the lion got up, roaring. But as he came near the barber, he began to purr and sat down. This was the same lion from which the barber had removed the thorn, and after so many years the lion recognised the barber and therefore did not attack him. The king said, "This fierce animal is not attacking him? What is this?" Then he thought, "Now I understand. Because I have made a mistake in arresting this man, the lion is not killing him. If the lion is not carrying out this punishment, then I also should not punish him." The king released the barber, showed him respect and asked for forgiveness.

Even in an animal there is so much gratitude, and Kṛṣṇadāsa Kavirāja Gosvāmī says that Nityānanda Prabhu's gratitude is just like this. For one minute that barber removed a thorn from the lion, and for so many years the lion remained grateful. That animal, which is so fierce that it kills innumerable other animals and people also, remained grateful for its entire life, and we see the same quality of gratitude in the life of Nityānanda Prabhu.

In *Śrī Caitanya-caritāmṛta*, Kṛṣṇadāsa Kavirāja Gosvāmī gives an example of how Nityānanda Prabhu, being Bhagavān Himself, is merciful to someone. He says that on one occasion there was to be a festival with *kīrtana* going on continuously all day and night. Vaiṣṇavas who lived both nearby and far away were invited, and they all came. Amongst them was an eternal associate of Nityānanda

Prabhu named Mīnaketana Rāmadāsa. His nature was such that his mercy could not be easily recognised, but those who understood him could see it. Generally, if some dear person comes, one offers *praṇāma*. But instead he would hit someone with the flute which he always kept in his hand, and that person would understand it to be great mercy. When he would place his foot on the head of someone, they would consider that there would be good fortune in their lives from that day on. Sometimes he would slap someone and say, "Where have you been all these days?" But those who understood knew that, "Whoever he has struck today will receive the direct mercy of Nityānanda Prabhu." So the *kīrtana* was going on, and when Mīnaketana Rāmadāsa came, everyone stood up, offered *praṇāma* to him, and welcomed him. He climbed on the shoulders of one person, hit another with his flute, and slapped another on the back. Tears were always flowing from his eyes, and he was always roaring out, "Nityānanda Prabhu *kī jaya*!"

The *pūjārī* there was somewhat educated, and when Mīnaketana Rāmadāsa entered, while everyone else had stood and offered praṇāma, this *pūjārī* didn't stand, and he also wouldn't speak to him. So, laughing, Mīnaketana Rāmadāsa said, "Here we find the second Romaharṣaṇa!", [1] and then he became absorbed in singing the glories of Nityānanda Prabhu. Everyone performed very loud *kīrtana*, and when it was finished, Kavirāja Gosvāmī's brother said, "You are always singing about the glories of Nityānanda

[1] Romaharṣaṇa is a personality who offended Baladeva Prabhu at a fire sacrifice being performed at Naimisaraṇya, as described in Chapter 78 of the Tenth Canto of *Śrīmad-Bhāgavatam*.

Prabhu, but why don't you sing the glories of Caitanya Mahāprabhu instead?" Hearing this, Mīnaketana Rāmadāsa became somewhat unhappy.

That man considered that there was some difference between Nityānanda Prabhu and Caitanya Mahāprabhu. But there are so many stories and glories of Nityānanda Prabhu, and they are all related to Caitanya Mahāprabhu. If someone is singing the glories of Śrīmatī Rādhikā, then are they not also singing the glories of Kṛṣṇa? Rādhikā is the dearmost of all to Kṛṣṇa, and Her service is the best of all. In singing the glories of Rādhikā, one must necessarily be glorifying Kṛṣṇa. And similarly, if someone is describing the glories of Caitanya Mahāprabhu, in doing so they cannot but be glorifying Śrī Rādhā and Kṛṣṇa.

Kavirāja Gosvāmī's brother continued, "Such a person you are: all the time chanting 'Nityānanda, Nityānanda,' and not glorifying Mahāprabhu. Always 'Nityānanda, Nityānanda,' but he married, whereas Mahāprabhu took *sannyāsa*, leaving His home and family."

Hearing this, Mīnaketana Rāmadāsa broke his flute and left that place. He was so unhappy that he broke his dear-most possession and left. At that time Kavirāja Gosvāmī thought to himself, "Now something inauspicious will certainly happen to my brother. How can there be any auspiciousness in his life after this?"

Gradually everything was destroyed for his brother. What do we mean by "destroyed"? His *bhakti* disappeared. By the mercy of saints one obtains *bhakti*, but if those saints are displeased, will our interest in *bhakti* remain? No. Everything was destroyed for him and he became an atheist, so Kavirāja Gosvāmī thought, "I will not keep company with such an atheist. I no longer consider him my brother. If one is not favourable towards *kṛṣṇa-bhakti*, then a friend is not a friend, a mother is not a mother, a father is not a father, and a relative is not a relative. I will not have any contact with him at all." Later that very night, at about three or four o'clock, he made the decision to leave, and very unhappily he went away from there.

Arriving at Jhamatpur village, Kavirāja Gosvāmī sat down to rest and began thinking, "I cannot stay here. Where will I go?" While thinking over his situation, he dozed off. Then Nityānanda Prabhu appeared to him in a dream. In his hand was a golden stick. His form was very large and had a glossy, dark lustre. He had an earring in one ear, and his beauty was marvellous, just like Baladeva's in *kṛṣṇa-līlā*. He said, "Why are you crying? Why are you upset? Get up, get up! Go to Vṛndāvana! And there place the feet of Rūpa and Sanātana on your head. Go! You left your brother for me? I am very pleased with you. A real brother is one who can give *bhakti*, a father is one who can give instructions regarding *bhakti*, and a mother is one who can inspire *kṛṣṇa-bhakti*. Your dear brother insulted me a little, and for that you left him forever? I am very pleased. Go to Vṛndāvana. There you will receive *darśana* of Govinda, Madana-mohana and Gopīnātha. You will receive the mercy of Rūpa and Sanātana, and also the mercy of Vṛndāvana-dhāma itself. Go!"

So Kavirāja Gosvāmī has written, "All I did was leave my brother, and for that Nityānanda Prabhu gave me such immense mercy! By that mercy, I have obtained *darśana* of Vṛndāvana-dhāma."

What kind of *darśana* did he obtain – like ours? This is the kind of *darśana* he received: he saw Kṛṣṇa taking the cows out to graze, the *gopīs* looking for Kṛṣṇa with thirsty eyes, and the *līlā* of Śrī Rādhā and Kṛṣṇa. And what is the meaning of the mercy of Rūpa and Sanātana? By Sanātana's mercy Kavirāja Gosvāmī obtained *sambandha-jñāna* and scriptural knowledge, but even when one possesses this knowledge, there still may not be *rasa*. By the mercy of Rūpa Gosvāmī he obtained the knowledge of *rasa*, and then he could compose such books as *Śrī Caitanya-caritāmṛta* and *Govinda-līlāmṛta*, wherein so much *rasa* is described. The mercy of Rūpa Gosvāmī has made all this possible.

In this world, even an animal will remain indebted for its entire life to someone who removes a thorn from it. In the same way, we are indebted to our *guru* and the Vaiṣṇavas. How can we be ungrateful to those who have tried to remove the thorn of material attachment from us, and have tried to entice us to drink *bhakti-rasa*? Towards such *gurus* and Vaiṣṇavas we should always be grateful. If on one day *gurudeva* is a little harsh with us and in one minute we become ungrateful, thinking, "Oh, he no longer has affection for me," what ill fortune that is. We will always remain indebted to *gurudeva* and the Vaiṣṇavas, and we can never repay this debt. If one doesn't understand this statement of Kṛṣṇadāsa Kavirāja, then that is his great misfortune; but one who understands this will never forget his indebtedness for his whole life. Even upon dying, he won't forget it, and then again in his next birth he will remember.

This gratitude is one of the main qualities of Bhagavān himself. Although Nityānanda Prabhu is Bhagavān himself, he becomes indebted to someone in the same way as Kṛṣṇa became indebted to the *gopīs*:

> *na pāraye 'haṁ niravadya-saṁyujāṁ*
> *sva-sādhu-kṛtyaṁ vibudhāyuṣāpi vaḥ*
> *yā mābhajan durjara-geha-śṛṅkhalāḥ*
> *saṁvṛścya tad vaḥ pratiyātu sādhunā*
>
> *Śrīmad-Bhāgavatam* (10.32.22)

Even within a long lifetime like that of the demigods I would be unable to repay you, because you have all left your homes and families to serve Me. Therefore please let your own glorious deeds be your compensation.

Similarly Nityānanda Prabhu says, "He has broken out of the shackles of material attachment and come to engage in my service. He doesn't care at all for worldly life. Can I ever leave those who have left their family, money and property to take up *bhajana*? I will never be able to."

Kavirāja Gosvāmī has also written:

> *saṅkarṣaṇaḥ kāraṇa-toya-śāyī*
> *garbhoda-śāyī ca payobdhi-śāyī*
> *śeṣaś ca yasyāṁśa-kalāḥ sa nityā-*
> *nandākhya-rāmaḥ śaraṇaṁ mamāstu*
>
> *Śrī Caitanya-caritāmṛta* (*Ādi-līlā* 5.7)

May Śrī Nityānanda Prabhu be my shelter. Saṅkarṣaṇa, Śeṣanāga, Kāraṇodakaśāyī Viṣṇu, Garbhodakaśāyī Viṣṇu and Kṣīrodakaśāyī Viṣṇu are His plenary portions and the portions of His plenary portions.

In Vaikuṇṭha there are different sections on the same level, and other sections that are on higher levels. Incarnations such as Nṛsiṁha, Kalki and Vāmana are on the same level in Vaikuṇṭha-dhāma. They share the same "floor" but have their own special chambers. The lowest point is the Virajā, then above that is Siddhaloka, which is known as the outside part of Vaikuṇṭha. Those enemies that are killed by Bhagavān are awarded that destination. Siddhaloka is also for those who chant *ahaṁ brahmāsmi*, thinking that the *jīva* ultimately merges into Brahman. But the *jīvas* cannot lose their individuality. That they ultimately become one is such a lie. Yes, they meet together, just as devotees meet together and share *hari-kathā*. As Kṛṣṇa comes together with the *gopīs*, *gopas*, Yaśodā and Nanda Bābā, and as Rāmacandra comes together with Hanumān – this meeting and coming together is done, but meeting and becoming one? Nowhere can such an example be found. Meeting, yes – but they will remain individual. The *jīva* never becomes Brahman. Many renowned *paṇḍitas* and scholars hold this theory and thousands of people come to hear their lectures. They say that there is nothing equal to *kṛṣṇa-bhakti* and that the *bhakti* of the *gopīs* is the best of all, and that anyone who attains devotion like that of the *gopīs* becomes one with Brahman. This type of *hari-kathā* is completely useless. They are deceiving people, and therefore we should not attend any functions where they say that we will become one with Rādhā-Kṛṣṇa.

Above Siddhaloka is Sadāśivaloka, and above that is Nārāyaṇa-dhāma, where the liberated four-armed devotees reside. *Sālokya*, *sāmīpya*, *sārūpya* and *sārṣṭi* – the devotees there possess these four kinds of liberation and remain near to Nārāyaṇa serving him in *aiśvarya-bhāva*, the mood of opulence. Nearby are millions of special chambers, and in them are Varāha, Nṛsiṁha, Kalki and all the other incarnations. When there is a necessity, they come to this world; otherwise they remain there all of the time, accepting service from their devotees. Above that is the world of Rāmacandra and above that is the world of Kṛṣṇa, which is known as Goloka. In calling this Goloka, there may be some confusion, so I will try to clarify it a little.

When Indra was performing the *abhiṣeka* of Kṛṣṇa, he brought Surabhi there. So the residence of Surabhi is Goloka, isn't it? But don't think that Indra brought her from Goloka Vṛndāvana. In this *brahmāṇḍa*, and each and every *brahmāṇḍa*, there is Hariloka, the residence of Kṣīrodakaśāyī Viṣṇu. The demigods cannot directly have Viṣṇu's *darśana*, but sometimes in his meditation Brahmā receives his *darśana* and attains the power to create and the strength to protect the world. In this way each *brahmāṇḍa* has its own Goloka, and this is also called Surabhiloka or Śvetadvīpa. Indra can travel up to there, and he brought Surabhi from there, saying, "You are *go-mātā*, so please pray to Kṛṣṇa for me."

Therefore this Goloka and Goloka Vṛndāvana are not one and the same. Similarly, the Navadvīpa-dhāma that is situated in the spiritual world is also known as Śvetadvīpa, but it is separate from the Śvetadvīpa included within this *brahmāṇḍa* wherein Kṣīrodakaśāyī Viṣṇu resides.

The lower section of Goloka-dhāma, below Dvārakā, is where there is *svakīya-bhāva*. Pastimes of Rādhā-Kṛṣṇa take place there, but there Rādhā-Kṛṣṇa are like extensions of Lakṣmī-Nārāyaṇa in the mood of opulence. This is the destination of those who perform *arcana* of Rādhā-Kṛṣṇa by *vaidhī-bhakti*. Those who perform *arcana* of Rādhā-Kṛṣṇa by *vaidhī-bhakti* combined with *rāgānugā* sentiments go to either Mathurā or Dvārakā. And those who have "greed" and fully follow *rāgānugā* in its pure form go to Goloka Vṛndāvana. That realm is in the shape of a lotus flower, and the centre of that lotus is the home of Nanda. Devotees who are fully absorbed in *rāgānuga-bhakti* attain positions there in the pastimes of Kṛṣṇa, either accompanying Kṛṣṇa as He takes the cows out to graze or as friends of Rādhikā. This is the highest attainment.

There Kṛṣṇa is known as Vṛndāvana-bihārī, Govinda, Śyāmasundara and Gopīnātha, and His first extension is Baladeva. Kṛṣṇa's stick, the peacock feather in Kṛṣṇa's crown, all of Kṛṣṇa's paraphernalia, the *gopīs'* paraphernalia, Vṛndāvana-dhāma – all of these are manifest by *sandhinī-śakti*, and the embodiment of that potency is Baladeva Prabhu. The embodiment of *hlādinī-śakti* is Rādhikā, and Kṛṣṇa is the possessor of *cit-śakti*. These three together are *sac-cid-ānanda*, the complete form of Kṛṣṇa. Neither Rādhikā nor Baladeva are separate from Him; together they are one.

From Baladeva Prabhu alone all the eternally perfected devotees of Kṛṣṇa are manifest. When Kṛṣṇa goes to Dvārakā, He becomes Vāsudeva, the son of Vasudeva. And in Dvārakā, Baladeva also feels that he is the son of Devakī, but in his original identity he is the son of Rohiṇī, and ultimately Nanda Bābā is Baladeva's father. Not that anyone can actually be the father of Baladeva as there are fathers and sons in this world, but Nanda Bābā has the identity of being his father. Nanda Bābā has the strongest identity of being the father of both Kṛṣṇa and Baladeva – ordinary, worldly scholars cannot accept this point. They cannot understand that in whomever the identity of being Kṛṣṇa's father is the most intense, that person is ultimately considered to be His father. Mostly they propound that Kṛṣṇa is the son of Vasudeva and very few of them accept that He is really Nanda-nandana.

Thus Baladeva Prabhu is the *vaibhava-prakāśa* of Kṛṣṇa, and he renders service to Kṛṣṇa all the time. Service to Kṛṣṇa is his everything, whether it is in Vṛndāvana, Mathurā or Dvārakā. When they go to Mathurā and Dvārakā, taking non-different forms, they become the first *catur-vyūha*: Vāsudeva, Saṇkarṣana, Pradyumna and Aniruddha. Then there is a second *catur-vyūha*, and from the root Saṅkarṣaṇa comes Mahā-Saṅkarṣaṇa. From Mahā-Saṅkarṣaṇa comes Kāraṇodakaśāyī Viṣṇu, from Kāraṇodakaśāyī comes Garbhodakaśāyī, and Garbhodakaśāyī becomes Kṣīrodakaśāyī. Kṣīrodakaśāyī Viṣṇu then expands into countless forms as the witness in the hearts of all living beings, Paramātmā. In our hearts, as the witness, is that very Baladeva in his *vyasti* (expansion) as the *antaryāmī* Kṣīrodakaśāyī. *Kṣīra* means milk, and just as our mother nourishes us by feeding us milk, he also sustains and nurtures us.

Near Kṣīrodakaśāyī Viṣṇu are Brahmā and Śaṇkara, and by his desire and power, creation and destruction of the material universes take place. As Śeṣanāga he has millions and millions of heads, and he is holding millions and millions of universes on his heads as if they were mustard seeds, while also taking the form of the beds on which all three *puruṣa-avatāras* lie. These are the six kinds of expansions of Baladeva Prabhu: from his original form in Vṛndāvana comes the root Saṅkarṣaṇa in Mathurā and Dvārakā, then Mahā-Saṅkarṣaṇa in Vaikuṇṭha, then Kāraṇodakaśāyī Viṣṇu, Garbhodakaśāyī Viṣṇu, Kṣīrodakaśāyī Viṣṇu and finally Śeṣa. One who knows these deep truths will never again have to enter the cycle of birth and death.

The *puruṣa-avatāra* is called *puruṣa* because he is related to the creation of the material world. He comes into contact with *māyā* indirectly for the purpose of creation and management, but he himself remains separate from it. Yes, he is inside all souls, but at the same time he is within no one. He does everything, and he inspires others to do everything, but simultaneously he does nothing. Therefore he is called a *puruṣa-avatāra*. From this *puruṣa-avatāra* come the *manvantara-avatāras*, *yuga-avatāras* and so many other incarnations. They come from Kāraṇodakaśāyī Viṣṇu or from Garbhodakaśāyī Viṣṇu, who can also be called *avatārī*, meaning that from them *avatāras* come forth.

When Kṛṣṇa comes to this world in any of His forms, then in the form of the *dhāma* and eternal associates, Baladeva Prabhu will certainly come also. Before Kṛṣṇa descends to perform pastimes in Vṛndāvana, Baladeva enters into the heart of Devakī and is present in her womb in the form of Saṅkarṣana; then Kṛṣṇa Himself can manifest. Therefore Baladeva comes first in the form of the *dhāma* and serves Kṛṣṇa in that way.

If someone says that Kṛṣṇa is an incarnation of Kāraṇodakaśāyī and someone else says that He is an incarnation of Garbhodakaśāyī, it will cause unnecessary confusion. In some places you will find such descriptions. Or sometimes Kṛṣṇa is described as being born from the hair of Nara-Nārāyaṇa – Keśa-avatāra, an incarnation of Nara-Nārāyaṇa. We may find such statements, but actually:

ete cāṁśa-kalāḥ puṁsaḥ
kṛṣṇas tu bhagavān svayam

Śrīmad-Bhāgavatam (1.3.28)

All the incarnations of Bhagavān are either plenary portions or parts of plenary portions of the *puruṣa-avatāras.* But Kṛṣṇa is Svayam Bhagavān Himself.

When it is said that Kṛṣṇa Himself is an incarnation, it is like a simple old lady who gives a blessing to the prime minister by saying, "My son, may you one day become the police commissioner." In her understanding, that is the highest post of all. The lady has said this with love, but she doesn't understand which position is higher. Similarly, some say that Kṛṣṇa is an incarnation of Garbhodakaśāyī or Kṣīrodakaśāyī Viṣṇu.

When Śrī Rāmacandra descended, Baladeva came as Lakṣmaṇa. Rāmacandra's pastimes are so full of separation and self-sacrifice that they make everyone cry. For apparently no reason, he deserted Sītā-devī, not only once, but twice. Lakṣmaṇa had not wanted Rāma to go to the forest, and therefore, while they were exiled, he said to Rāma, "I no longer consider Mahārāja Daśaratha to be our father. Being excessively lusty, he is controlled by a woman; and in his old age his intelligence has diminished. I should kill him! Look – someone is coming! If it is Bharata, I will kill him also!"

Bharata was coming to appease Rāma, but when Lakṣmaṇa climbed up a tree and saw the armies, he became very angry. Taking his bow and arrow, he started towards them. "Where are you going?" Rāma asked. "With whom will you fight?"

Lakṣmaṇa said, "Bharata has come with great pride. He wants to remove you so there will be no obstacle to him becoming the king! Therefore I am going now, and with one arrow I will finish them all!"

But Rāma was thinking that there was a misunderstanding, so he told Lakṣmaṇa a story. Once there was a woman who raised a mongoose for the purpose of protecting her household from snakes. Each day, she put her children to sleep on the bed and, placing the mongoose nearby, went out. One day, while she was out, a snake came desiring to bite the children. The mongoose had a great fight with the snake, and with great difficulty the mongoose killed it and protected the children. Then, being pleased with itself, the mongoose was waiting outside the house for its mistress, and there was still some blood on its mouth from the fight. The woman returned, and the mongoose went before her, saying "ku-ku-ku". The woman said, "Where has this blood come from? You attacked the children and harmed them?" Hastily, she picked up a stick and killed the mongoose. Then she went inside the house and saw the children playing; the dead snake was laying nearby. Realising her mistake, she lamented.

So Rāma said to Lakṣmaṇa, "Your condition is exactly like this. First wait and see; let Bharata come. Even the Earth herself can be selfish, but Bharata can never be selfish.

Nowhere in this world is there an emblem of love like Bharata. So let him come."

When Bharata came, he fell at the feet of Rāma and began to appease him. Seeing him offering *praṇāma* to Rāma, Lakṣmaṇa realised his mistake. When Bharata was leaving, Lakṣmaṇa approached him alone and fell at his feet. As Bharata lifted him up and embraced him, Lakṣmaṇa said, "I am a great offender at your feet. I have not been able to be affectionate to you, to love you," and he began weeping bitterly.

Another time during the period when they were living in the forest, Rāma ordered Lakṣmaṇa to bring wood when Sītā desired to enter the fire. Lakṣmaṇa became very angry, but Rāma said, "Service rendered in the forest is the highest. You are always a servant." Lakṣmaṇa accepted the order of Rāma but thought, "I am making a mistake following his order." So he brought wood, and Sītā-devī entered into the fire. Of course this was a pretext by which the real Sītā came out and the false Sītā disappeared, but still, in the end, Lakṣmaṇa took a vow that, "I will not come again as your younger brother, but only as your older brother. Then things will be different, and you will not be able to treat me like this."

Therefore in the pastimes of Kṛṣṇa he came as Baladeva, and in the pastimes of Mahāprabhu he came as Nityānanda Prabhu, the older brother both times. So many pastimes could be performed only as an older brother, which from the position of a younger brother would not be possible. If Nityānanda Prabhu were not present, then so many of Mahāprabhu's pastimes would have remained hidden. He was Mahāprabhu's servant, His brother and His *guru* also. How was he Mahāprabhu's *guru*? Mahāprabhu's *guru* was Īśvara Purī, the *guru* of Īśvara Purī was Mādhavendra Purī and the *guru* of Mādhavendra Purī was Lakṣmīpati Tīrtha. Nityānanda Prabhu was also a disciple of Lakṣmīpati Tīrtha, but because his *guru* departed from this world when he was at a young age, Nityānanda Prabhu received nearly all of his instruction from Mādhavendra Purī. Whoever gives instruction on *bhakti* is the representative of Bhagavān, and therefore Nityānanda Prabhu always considered Mādhavendra Purī to be his primary *guru*. When Mādhavendra Purī became his *guru*, then Īśvara Purī became his godbrother, and since Nityānanda Prabhu was therefore on the level of Mahāprabhu's *guru*, Mahāprabhu respected him in that way.

Although we see that Nityānanda Prabhu had three relationships with Mahāprabhu – as a servant, a brother and a *guru* – still, Nityānanda Prabhu always considered himself a servant. When Mahāprabhu was absorbed in *kīrtana*, generally it was Nityānanda Prabhu who protected Him. When Mahāprabhu was dancing in His usual way, Nityānanda Prabhu would catch Him for His own protection, and only when Mahāprabhu became absorbed in *rādhā-bhāva* could Nityānanda Prabhu not touch Him. Nityānanda Prabhu would engage in all types of service, always following the order of Mahāprabhu. Mahāprabhu told him, "Please go to Bengal! The *brāhmaṇas* there, being very proud, don't perform *bhajana* of Bhagavān. Preach something to the *brāhmaṇa* class, but mostly preach to those who are considered fallen in society, because they are not really fallen.

Each and every soul has the right to perform *bhagavad-bhajana*. Please go." So Nityānanda Prabhu went there, preached from village to village, and made disciples of everyone.

Once, Nityānanda Prabhu was going along the road with a preaching party when they came across a village where there lived a wealthy landowner named Rāmacandra Khān. Nityānanda Prabhu entered the man's home and sat down on the altar of the *durgā-maṇḍapa*. Previously in Bengal the wealthy people would have such *maṇḍapas* (canopies raised for ceremonial purposes) for Caṇḍī, or Durgā. He was thinking, "Night is falling, so where can we possibly go now? Tomorrow morning we will continue on our way."

Meanwhile Rāmacandra Khān sent one of his servants to speak to Nityānanda Prabhu. Sarcastically the man said, "There is not enough space for you here in the house, but we have a *gośālā* which is a very pure place due to the presence of cows and cow dung. Saints and *sādhus* should stay there, so go to the *gośālā*."

When Nityānanda Prabhu heard this, he became angry and said, "Yes, you are right. This place is unfit for me. It is fit for cow-killing meat-eaters." Saying this, he left that place. The next day Muslims attacked and arrested Rāmacandra Khān and his entire family. They also killed a cow, cooked the meat and ate it on that very spot. The entire village was destroyed.

Nityānanda Prabhu has two aspects, just like a mother lion. To her cubs the lion is very kind, but to others she is very dangerous. Similarly Nityānanda Prabhu is supremely merciful to the devotees and is the subduer of atheists. Just as Baladeva Prabhu holds a plough and club and killed Dvivida gorilla and others who were inimical to Kṛṣṇa, Nityānanda Prabhu subdues the atheists and increases *gaura-prema* in devotees.

We should never consider there to be any difference between Caitanya Mahāprabhu and Nityānanda Prabhu; there is a difference in body only. Nityānanda Prabhu is the complete *guru-tattva*, and wherever there is *guru*, he is there. Wherever the activities of *guru* are performed, the message of Kṛṣṇa is given to the *jīvas* that by *bhakti* only will there be real auspiciousness. This is all manifested by Nityānanda Prabhu. Therefore on this day we offer *praṇāma* unto he who is the most merciful and the complete *guru-tattva*, and we pray that he will always be merciful to us.

Chapter Nine

Simply a Quality of Bhakti

Bhagavān has ordered that we should never give any importance to whatever faults may be seen in the bodies or natures of devotees who are engaged in His exclusive *bhajana*. We should not criticise them, be envious of them, or consider them to be of poor conduct. Suppose there is a man who never lies, steals or engages in any misconduct but doesn't perform exclusive *bhajana* of Bhagavān. Then there is another man who performs exclusive *bhajana* of Bhagavān and has *ruci* for taking *harināma* and hearing *hari-kathā*, but some bad qualities or physical deformities can be detected in him. How should we view these two men? Between them who is superior? The *Bhagavad-gītā* states that the one who performs *bhajana* is the best. But ordinarily people are not taught this. What to speak of others, even Sītā, who is Lakṣmī-devī herself, was not accepted by the residents of Ayodhyā after Rāvaṇa had taken her to his abode in Śrī Laṅkā. Rāma said, "No, she is pure; she will stay with me in the palace." But even though she was actually the most exalted personality in Ayodhyā, they sent her away without any remorse.

These conventions still exist today. If we see some external fault in a person, we disregard them. These days almost everyone sees with mundane vision. They don't see the tendency of *bhakti* inside others; they only see external things and then judge others on these considerations. Only those who have had abundant association with *sādhus*, who are higher-level *madhyama-adhikārī* Vaiṣṇavas, whose *anarthas* have disappeared, and who are approaching the *uttama-adhikārī* stage, will honour what Kṛṣṇa has said regarding this point. And everyone else, who possess only mundane intelligence, will say, "Oh, this devotee is not of good conduct and is therefore a hypocrite." They also do not properly respect Nārada because he said, "There is no need for us to understand what is religiosity and irreligiosity." There is also no necessity to honour worldly conventions. What is our only necessity? *Bhakti* – exclusive *prema-bhakti* for Kṛṣṇa is our only objective, and our firm resolution is that besides this there is no other meaning to life.

sva-pāda-mūlaṁ bhajataḥ priyasya
tyaktānya-bhāvasya hariḥ pareśaḥ
vikarma yac cotpatitaṁ kathañcid
dhunoti sarvaṁ hṛdi sanniviṣṭaḥ

Śrīmad-Bhāgavatam (11.5.42)

If someone has left their family, wife, children, money, all worldly attachments and enjoyments, and is engaged in the exclusive *bhajana* of Bhagavān, but somehow or other he performs some sinful activity, then Bhagavān, being situated within that person's heart, at once forgives him. But if there is a person of good conduct who has spoken the truth throughout his entire life, who has engaged in welfare activities for society and for people in general, who has worshipped the demigods and endeavoured for liberation, but has never engaged in *bhagavad-bhajana*, then what real benefit has there been for him? And if a devotee falls from the path of *bhajana* in an immature stage, what is the loss for him?

śucīnāṁ śrīmatāṁ gehe
yoga-bhraṣṭo 'bhijāyate

Bhagavad-gītā (6.41)

In his next life he will take birth in a pure or wealthy family where there are devotees, and he will naturally be attracted to *bhakti* again. And for the other man who didn't perform any *bhajana*? There is no real benefit for him. Only to the degree that one can give his heart to *bhajana* will he be benefited. So only a *madhyama-adhikārī* Vaiṣṇava will be able to place emphasis on the *bhakti* in others rather than on external considerations.

yadi kuryāt pramādena
yogī karma vigarhitam
yogenaiva dahed aṁho
nānyat tatra kadācana

Śrīmad-Bhāgavatam (11.20.25)

If an ordinary *yogī* somehow falls from his practice, he will be finished. But if a *bhakti-yogī* accidentally commits some detestable activity, then by his very practice of *bhakti-yoga* he will again be set right. For him there is no need of any other procedure. Continuing to take *harināma* will be his only atonement. Devotees are not intentionally sinful, so therefore for them there is no need of atonement. What has happened has happened, but deliberately they wouldn't commit sins. Kṛṣṇa always forgives those who have *bhakti* for Him and He makes their hearts pure in all ways.

ajñāne vā haya yadi 'pāpa' upasthita
kṛṣṇa tāṅre śuddha kare, nā karāya prāyaścitta

Śrī Caitanya-caritāmṛta (*Madhya-līlā* 22.143)

If a devotee accidentally commits some sinful activity, there is no need for him to undergo any atonement. By continuing his practice of *bhakti*, his heart will be purified. Those who know the *tattva* of *bhagavad-bhakti* say that by the devotee's continuing to take *harināma* all impurities will leave him.

māṁ hi pārtha vyapāśritya
ye 'pi syuḥ pāpa-yonayaḥ
striyo vaiśyās tathā śūdrās
te 'pi yānti parāṁ gatim

Bhagavad-gītā (9.32)

[Śrī Kṛṣṇa said:] O son of Pṛthā, those who take shelter of Me, though they be of lower birth – women, merchants and manual labourers – can attain the supreme destination.

Pāpa-yonayaḥ means those who are sinful by birth. *Śrīmad-Bhāgavatam* (2.4.18) has listed some of these classes: Kirāta, Hūṇa, Āndhra. Kirāta live in the jungle and kill and eat the flesh of animals and birds, even pigeons. They keep goats, sheep and pigs, and after fattening them up, they slaughter them and eat their flesh. Yavana, Khasa and all similar tribes do this. They are sinful from birth to death. Actually, for them eating meat is nothing; they don't even have any conventions such as marriage for relationships between men and women! From birth they eat meat, drink liquor and freely unite with women. *Striyo* means women. Though some are chaste, these days most women are unchaste. And the *śūdras* kill the cow, eat its flesh and use its skin to make shoes. *Te 'pi yānti paraṁ gatim*: even these people can attain the supreme destination through executing *bhagavad-bhakti*, so what to speak of those who engage in exclusive devotion but may have accidentally fallen?

If one engages in *bhakti-sādhana* and takes shelter of *harināma* and hearing *hari-kathā*, then birth after birth the result from that will never be destroyed, as long as there has been no *vaiṣṇava-aparādha*. The seed of *bhakti* is within that *sādhaka*. Birth after birth his *sukṛti* will become stronger and stronger, and eventually he will attain *para-bhakti*. For those who have some special eagerness, it may even be possible in only two or three births. Bhagavān will lead us to Him – either today, or after ten, twenty or one thousand births He will eventually lead us to Him, as long as the seed within us has not been destroyed. And there is only one thing that does that – *aparādha* towards the *guru* or Vaiṣṇavas.

The *jīva* has independence, and by misuse of this independence he becomes implicated in the reactions to his own misdeeds. If by this independence one has blasphemed or offended any Vaiṣṇava, then that is due to the uncontrolled mind. We should never offend a Vaiṣṇava because from the *śakti* of *guru* and Vaiṣṇavas we will get the mercy of Bhagavān. What determines if we will do *bhajana* or not do *bhajana*? Whose desire determines this? Bhagavān's? No, it is ours only. If we simply take up *bhajana*, then *guru* and the Vaiṣṇavas will be merciful and give us the necessary strength to achieve the direct mercy of Bhagavān. But first of all the desire must come from within us. And if while engaging in *bhajana*, the desires for prestige and wealth exist within us, should we think that Bhagavān put them there? "I am doing just as Bhagavān inspires me" – we shouldn't think like this in regard to *anarthas*. Those things are due solely to our own weakness. If we are unable to absorb our minds in *bhagavad-bhajana*, whose fault is that? Ours only, and not Bhagavān's. Don't think that "Bhagavān is doing this to me." Bhagavān is merely bestowing the reactions to our own activities. Reactions to our previous pious and sinful activities will come, and we will feel some difficulty because of them. So it is correct to think that He is bestowing the fruits of our *karma*, but otherwise He has no direct relationship with our difficulties.

If a devotee who practises exclusive *bhajana* is struck by a serious disease, why has it happened? It is a reaction to the sins of his previous lives. But sometimes Bhagavān will even put such an apparent obstacle in a *sādhaka's* path in order to curb his pride. He may try to increase that devotee's humility by this means. Therefore, beware! Don't think ill of another devotee because some fault may appear in his body or in his nature. If we maintain such an attitude towards devotees who are engaged in exclusive *bhajana*, we will be expelled from the kingdom of *bhakti*. We should consider all of these points and understand their importance in our pursuit of *bhakti*. If someone is lame, blind, a Kirāta, Āndhra, Pulinda or whatever, but has become a devotee, then Bhagavān will bestow upon him all good qualities and eventually take him up to Vaikuṇṭha. Therefore we should never harbour any ill feelings towards anyone who practises exclusive *bhajana*. And one who behaves nicely, who has a very attractive appearance and who has taken birth in a *brāhmaṇa* family but doesn't engage in *bhajana* – it is all useless and his life has no meaning. Don't think that this is an astonishing thing; it is simply a quality of *bhakti*.

According to their natures some people may have many faults, but we should always place emphasis on their *bhakti* instead. It is not that an ill-behaved person cannot take the name of Bhagavān, cannot do *bhajana* or cannot hear *hari-kathā*. And it is not that only those who have taken birth within the *brāhmaṇa*, *kṣatriya*, *vaiśya* and *śūdra* classes can take *harināma*. Whatever condition one is in, even if he is as sinful as Ajāmila was, he can chant Bhagavān's name and hear *hari-kathā*, and in this way become qualified to always remember Him.

Kirāta, Āndhra, Pulinda, Śumbha, Yavana – these are all sinful classes of people from the time of the *Bhāgavatam*. They still exist today but in different forms. They all originate from the Hindu lineage. All of the people that we see in India today, whether they are Muslims, Christians, Buddhists or Jains, all had the same source: Brahmā. So originally there was only one class of humans, but some degraded and became sinful by nature. In Āssām there is a class of people who smoke different varieties of hemp with a water-pipe. Anytime there is some important task to be accomplished, they first all get together and smoke. They even engage their children in smoking, so they are sinful from birth. Others may take a good birth but become sinful later in life. If either of these classes of sinful people associate with *sādhus* and take shelter of a *guru*, they can be purified and their faults will be destroyed.

But will they be able to leave all those faults at once? If we see that someone is worshipping several demigods and goddesses, and we say to him, "My friend, don't worship Durgā at this time of Navarātri. Instead worship Kṛṣṇa," then they will not come in our direction. Therefore we should just let them come with whatever conceptions they may have, and after they have sat and heard something three or four times, it will start to become natural for them. Even if they are sometimes drinking wine, we should think nothing of it. Such a thing is written in the *Bhāgavatam*:

loke vyavāyāmiṣa-madya-sevā
nityā hi jantor na hi tatra codanā
vyavasthitis teṣu vivāha-yajña-
surā-grahair āsu nivṛttir iṣṭā

Śrīmad-Bhāgavatam (11.5.11)

It is not proper to drink liquor, but if a newcomer takes a little wine at the time of a marriage or a festival, we should think nothing of it. After hearing more and more *hari-kathā*, they will automatically give up these bad habits. But in the very beginning the practice of strict *bhakti-sādhana* doesn't always come naturally.

aho bata śva-paco 'to garīyān
yaj-jihvāgre vartate nāma tubhyam
tepus tapas te juhuvuḥ sasnur āryā
brahmānūcur nāma gṛnanti ye te

Śrīmad-Bhāgavatam (3.33.7)

[Devahūti said to Kapiladeva:] How glorious are they whose tongues are chanting your holy name! Even if they were born in the families of dog-eaters, such persons are worshipful. Those who chant your holy name must have performed all kinds of austerities and fire sacrifices, bathed at holy places of pilgrimage, studied the Vedas and become fully qualified in all ways."

For one who has *ruci* for chanting the name of Bhagavān and for hearing *hari-kathā*, there is no necessity to perform any separate austerities or sacrifices or to study the Vedas. Even if his behaviour is opposed to Vedic principles, people ordinarily think that his *bhakti* will be destroyed, but it is not necessarily so.

In the first part of *Śrī Bṛhad-bhāgavatāmṛta*, there is a section where Nārada and Hanumān are conversing. Upon hearing how dear Draupadī, Arjuna and all the Pāṇḍavas are to Kṛṣṇa, Nārada became very pleased and began dancing. Hanumān also danced with great happiness. In such devotees there are no reservations or feelings of shyness; their *ānanda* increased as they discussed this topic and naturally they began dancing. Hanumān proposed that Nārada should go to Hastināpura to have *darśana* of the Pāṇḍavas and then spoke this verse:

bṛhad-vrata-dharān asmāṁs
taṁś ca gārhasthya-dharmiṇaḥ
samrāya-vyāpṛtan matvā
māparādha-vṛto bhava

Bṛhad-bhāgavatamāmṛta (1.4.114)

Please don't commit the offence of thinking that we are *naiṣṭhika-brahmacārīs*, whereas the Pāṇḍavas are mere *gṛhasthas* busy in managing a kingdom.

Those who have the firm resolution to never become householders are called *naiṣṭhika-brahmacārīs*. From following this vow comes the qualification to follow *sannyāsa-dharma*. The other type of *brahmacārī* is called *upakurvāṇa*. They remain in white cloth and serve as *brahmacārīs*, but those who desire to do so can return to their homes and marry. Kṛṣṇa and Balarāma were *upakurvāṇa-brahmacārīs* because after studying under their *guru*, they returned to their home. Śukadeva Gosvāmī, Nārada, the Kumāras and Hanumān never married and were *naiṣṭhika-brahmacārīs*. Vyāsadeva, Janaka Mahārāja and Ambarīṣa Mahārāja were all *upakurvāṇa-brahmacārīs* who returned to their homes and performed *bhajana* there.

Nārada was a *naiṣṭhika-brahmacārī* who had renounced everything and didn't accumulate anything at all, whereas the Pāṇḍavas were followers of *gṛhastha-dharma* engaged in managing the affairs of a kingdom; so between them, who is superior? If Nārada goes to the palace of the Pāṇḍavas, who will offer *praṇāma* to whom? The Pāṇḍavas will offer *praṇāma* to Nārada, even though their *bhakti* is higher than his, because they will honour the regulations of their *āśrama* as defined within the *varṇāśrama* system. Similarly, when Caitanya Mahāprabhu was a young *sannyāsī* and went to the place of Vallabhācārya, who was approximately ninety years old and conversant in all the *śāstras*, Mahāprabhu fell at his feet. Mahāprabhu behaved in the same fashion with Advaita Ācārya, but internally Advaita Prabhu respected Mahāprabhu as his master.

So Hanumān was saying that it is not proper to analyse whether one is a *brahmacārī* or a *gṛhastha* because we may become offenders. One who possesses the most *prema* for Bhagavān is superior, and being a *gṛhastha* is no obstacle to this. And even in some situations, without becoming a *gṛhastha*, loving feelings towards Bhagavān will not come. For example, a *gopī* will not be able to have *parakīya-bhāva* in *kṛṣṇa-līlā* without becoming married. But marrying is not necessary for *vaidhī-bhakti*, and it is not beneficial for *rāgānuga-bhakti* either. Rūpa and Sanātana Gosvāmīs were *naiṣṭhika-brahmacārīs*, but will a *naiṣṭhika-brahmacārī* ever take employment in a kingdom as they did? So even though in the strictest sense we can't say they were really *naiṣṭika-brahmacārīs*, they were endowed with millions of transcendental qualities and were real *paramahaṁsas*.

Therefore Hanumān is saying that one should not minimise the position of the Pāṇḍavas just because they are *gṛhasthas* and are always busy in managing the affairs of a kingdom. Yudhiṣṭhira Mahārāja is an emperor, why? For the preaching of *bhakti*. Why does he have a relationship with Draupadī? Because she is very dear to Śrī Kṛṣṇa. Why is he so fond of Arjuna? Because Arjuna is the dear friend of Kṛṣṇa. Therefore we should never minimise the position of Yudhiṣṭhira. He has three relationships with Kṛṣṇa: as His *guru*, meaning that he has affection for Kṛṣṇa just as a father would, as His friend and as His servant. We shouldn't think less of any of the Pāṇḍavas, because they all have their own glorious relationship with Bhagavān. Kuntī gave birth to them, and through them the glories of *kṛṣṇa-bhakti* were spread throughout the world. Also, every part of Draupadī's life is full of *prema-bhakti* for Kṛṣṇa.

Therefore we mustn't consider that just because one is

a *naiṣṭhika-brahmacārī* he must be necessarily given more respect than a *gṛhastha*. The calibre of *bhakti* in a person is the important thing, whether they be a *sannyāsī*, *brahmacārī*, *gṛhastha*, woman, prostitute, dog-eater or whatever.

Chapter Ten

From Bhaktivinoda Ṭhākura's
Śrī Bhajana-rahasya

(1)

From Bhaktivinoda Ṭhākura's Śrī *Bhajana-rahasya*, we will discuss the first stage of *bhajana*, which is called *śraddhā*.

guru-kṛṣṇa-prasāde pāya bhakti-latā-bīja

Śrī Caitanya-caritāmṛta (*Madhya-līlā* 19.151)

By the mercy of *guru* and Kṛṣṇa the seed of the creeper of *bhakti* is bestowed upon a fortunate soul.

Śraddhā means faith in the teachings of *guru*, Vaiṣṇavas and *śāstra*. Here we are not speaking on whether someone is sincerely engaged in *bhajana* or not, or whether they have overcome their *anarthas* or not. Before that consideration can come, a neophyte devotee must possess the *śraddhā* that "I will do as my *guru*, the Vaiṣṇavas and the scriptures instruct me." Then in sequence he will progress through the different stages on the devotional path. Besides *sādhu-saṅga* there is no other way of receiving the seed of the *bhakti* creeper. This seed comes exclusively from hearing the words of a *sādhu*. First of all there will be *śraddhā*, then one will engage in *sādhana-bhakti*, and then so many devotional activities will be performed – taking shelter at the feet of a *guru*, accepting instruction from him, serving him intimately and performing all the other limbs of *bhakti*. But first there must be *sādhu-saṅga*, and as that increases in quality, *śraddhā* towards *kṛṣṇa-nāma* will arise. At first there won't be *niṣṭhā* (firm resolution in *sādhana*), but some faith will be there. When that faith becomes of good quality, one will understand that in the age of Kali there is no other method for spiritual success besides taking *kṛṣṇa-nāma*, and that this method will enable one to cross over the ocean of material existence and attain the direct service of Bhagavān. Besides taking the name of Bhagavān there is no other way – performing austerities, following vows, travelling to holy places, or whatever – they are all secondary, and performing them alone will not enable one to cross over the ocean of material existence and fully please Bhagavān.

Therefore the sole method is the chanting of the name of Bhagavān; this is the instruction given by Śrī Caitanya Mahāprabhu. And amongst all the names of Bhagavān, in Kali-yuga the *mahā-mantra* is the topmost. Entering the garden of Bhagavān's names, Caitanya Mahāprabhu specially selected *kṛṣṇa-nāma* as the most beautiful, fragrant, soft and sweet *nāma*, and threading these names together as the garland of the *mahā-mantra*, He bestowed it upon the *jīvas*. He bestowed it upon whoever came across His path: "Hare Kṛṣṇa, Hare Kṛṣṇa, Kṛṣṇa Kṛṣṇa, Hare Hare, Hare Rāma, Hare Rāma, Rāma Rāma, Hare Hare." Bhaktivinoda Ṭhākura says that for ordinary people and for new *sādhakas*, this is who is being addressed by each name within the *mahā-mantra*: "O Hari, O Kṛṣṇa, O Hari, O Kṛṣṇa, O Kṛṣṇa, O Kṛṣṇa, O Hari, O Hari, O Hari, O Rāma, O Hari,

O Rāma, O Rāma, O Rāma, O Hari, O Hari." In the chanting of these names there is no consideration of time, place or circumstance. Anyone can chant these names. But as one follows the process and advances, he will take shelter of the feet of a *guru*, hear *hari-kathā* from him, and continue taking *harināma*. Then his *anarthas* will begin to dissipate and for him the meaning of these names will change. He will begin to feel that Hare means Śrīmatī Rādhikā who steals away the heart of Kṛṣṇa, and then, when chanting the *mahā-mantra*, this is who he will be calling: "O Rādhā, O Kṛṣṇa, O Rādhā, O Kṛṣṇa, O Kṛṣṇa, O Kṛṣṇa, O Rādhā, O Rādhā, O Rādhā, O Rādhā-ramaṇa, O Rādhā, O Rādhā-ramaṇa, O Rādhā-ramaṇa, O Rādhā-ramaṇa, O Rādhā, O Rādhā." Then the full meaning of the *mantra* will continue to bloom until one arrives at the stage of *bhāva*. In Jagannātha Purī, Gopāla-guru and his disciple Dhyānacandra heard instructions from Caitanya Mahāprabhu and Svarūpa Dāmodara that made them realise this meaning of the *mahā-mantra*. And through Raghunātha dāsa Gosvāmī a more special meaning manifested. Meditating on this meaning one should chant *harināma-japa* and *kīrtana* and thereby progress steadily upwards.

The beginning stages of *sādhana* have been compared to the darkness of night. If you try to walk anywhere in the darkness, you may stumble or step into a ditch or even upon a snake, so there is some fear. Or if you enter a jungle you may be attacked by a tiger or lion. There are also thieves and dacoits to be wary of. Thieves don't come in the first part of the night because at that time most people have just settled in and can be easily awakened, but they come nearer to morning when most people are in deep sleep. There are also such thieves and fearful adversaries in the beginning stages of *bhajana*. At this point the stars in the evening sky have not yet disappeared, meaning lust, anger, greed, envy and madness have not disappeared from our hearts. Our many *anarthas*, which have been compared to tigers and snakes, are hidden in all directions. But will the practice of *sādhana* alone make the sun of spiritual perfection rise? When does the sun rise? When the appropriate time comes, and not before. So here one thing is possible: if a lamp is lit in the night, then snakes and other fearful adversaries will flee. It is the *guru* who lights this lamp for us by giving us *harināma* and making us hear *hari-kathā*. Then the *anarthas* which remain within us will begin to fade, but is that alone enough to make the sun rise? The sun of full realisation of the holy name will rise according to its own sweet will; it is fully independent.

ataḥ śrī-kṛṣṇa-nāmādi
na bhaved grāhyam indriyaiḥ
sevonmukhe hi jihvādau
svayam eva sphuraty adaḥ

Bhakti-rasāmṛta-sindhu (1.2.234)

The material senses cannot perceive the names, form, qualities and pastimes of Śrī Kṛṣṇa. Only when one is fully absorbed in serving Him does the real *nāma* appear on one's tongue, bestowing full realisation of Him.

Just as the sun rises at precisely the appropriate time, when the time is right the holy name will appear on a devotee's tongue and illuminate everything within his heart. And just as when the sun rises there is no need of any electric light or candle because everything is automatically illuminated, when the holy name bestows full realisation upon a devotee, he will have a clear understanding of himself in his constitutional position, and all of his fear will vanish.

'eka' kṛṣṇa-nāme kare sarva-pāpa nāśa
premera kāraṇa bhakti karena prakāśa

Śrī Caitanya-caritāmṛta (*Ādi-līlā* 8.26)

Simply chanting *kṛṣṇa-nāma* without offences vanquishes all sinful activities, and thus *bhakti*, which is the cause of *prema*, becomes manifest.

By its mercy the holy name will fully reveal itself, but as long as it hasn't arisen in the heart, we can only endeavour to make the darkness go away, meaning we must continue executing *sādhana* in an effort to rid ourselves of our *anarthas*.

Next Bhaktivinoda Ṭhākura says that after one accepts a *guru* and the seed of the creeper of *bhakti* is planted in his heart, the seed must be carefully cultivated and then a seedling will appear. *Ceto-darpaṇa-mārjanam* – slowly the devotee's consciousness is being purified. The holy name is completely *sac-cid-ānanda* – it is not a material vibration. We cannot manipulate it or control it in any way; perhaps *premī* devotees can overpower it, but in our present condition we cannot. We have been bound by *māyā* since time immemorial. We have been wandering in the material realm sometimes as kings, sometimes as demigods, sometimes as insects, and in many other species also. Wandering and wandering, by the causeless mercy of Bhagavān we attain the company of Vaiṣṇavas. One who has merit from previous lifetimes will automatically attain very high quality Vaiṣṇava association, and upon hearing their *hari-kathā*, his *anarthas* will at once disappear and he will swiftly enter into *bhakti*. But for one who doesn't have this previous merit, there will be some delay. Still, he should remain patient and continue performing *sādhana* in the company of Vaiṣṇavas, because whether the *śraddhā* that has arisen in one's heart is based on scriptural regulations or of the nature of pure spiritual greed, one must always remain in *sādhu-saṅga*.

The *jīva* is covered by a material body and a subtle body, and as long as they remain, he thinks "I am this body" or "I am mind, intelligence and ego." Because *bhagavan-nāma* is transcendental, it does not manifest to the material senses. However, if one becomes fully pure, then the sun of the holy name will arise in his heart. But in our present condition everything is material – our bodies, our minds, everything we do and say – so how will this transcendental, *sac-cid-ānanda bhagavan-nāma* appear in our hearts? Regarding this point, Bhaktivinoda Ṭhākura says, "Listen to the method." First one receives *sādhu-saṅga*, and then he accepts a *guru*, but that doesn't just mean going through the ritual of initiation. "Whatever Gurujī says, I will certainly do" – one must have this determination, and for that three things are necessary: *paripraśnena* (sincere inquiry), *praṇipātena* (submission) and *sevayā* (service attitude). With these three things we will begin hearing from the *guru*. Gurujī will say, "Listen! You must overcome your *anarthas*."

Then the disciple will ask, "Gurujī, what are *anarthas*?"

Gurujī says, "That which has no *artha* (value), which is

not beneficial to our very selves, the soul, is called an *anartha*."

"Gurujī, please explain it in more detail. I have not completely understood."

"Then listen attentively – I will also tell you how you can eradicate them."

māyā-mugdhasya jīvasya
jñeyo 'narthaś catur-vidhaḥ
hṛd-daurbalyaṁ cāparādho
'sat-tṛṣṇā tattva-vibhramaḥ

Śrī Bhajana-rahasya (2.7)

Having *prema* for Bhagavān is our original *artha*, that which is our real wealth. *Kṛṣṇa-prema* is our objective, and within this *kṛṣṇa-prema*, *rādhā-dāsya* is our ultimate objective. This is our *artha*, and that which hinders and obscures this is called an *anartha*. There are four kinds of them, and the first is called *svarūpa-bhrama* – being in illusion concerning what our inherent form is, and what the form of *para-tattva*, Bhagavān, is. Some say, "I am Brahman" or "I am Bhagavān." Others say that Indra is Bhagavān, and others say that Gaṇeśa is Bhagavān. Others say, "Both Indra and Gaṇeśa are Brahman, as are me, you, your wife and children, and everyone else in the universe: *sarvaṁ khalv idaṁ brahma*. Since we are all Brahman, is there any necessity of engaging in *bhajana*? There is no necessity of it whatsoever." This is all *bhrama*, illusion. Therefore one must first understand, "Who am I?" One should rid himself of the first stage of illusion, which is thinking that he is the physical body. Then he will realise that the activities which he has been busily engaged in from dawn to dusk are all *anartha*. Understanding *ātma-tattva* means to realise that one is an eternal servant of Kṛṣṇa. And who is *para-tattva*? Not Brahman, not even Paramātmā, but only Kṛṣṇa, who is our supreme *artha*. This understanding is our everything:

ete cāṁśa-kalāḥ puṁsaḥ
kṛṣṇas tu bhagavān svayam

Śrīmad-Bhāgavatam (1.3.28)

Kṛṣṇa is Bhagavān Himself – this is *para-tattva*. And what is His nature? He is *sarva-śaktimān*, the possessor of all potencies, who can make the impossible possible. Why should we worship Gaṇeśa, Brahmā or Śaṅkara when they themselves worship Kṛṣṇa? And in what forms do we worship Kṛṣṇa? As Madana-mohana, Govinda and Gopīnātha – these three are one *tattva*. As Madana-mohana He establishes our *sambandha* (eternal relationship), as Govinda He accepts our service and then as Gopīnātha He bestows our *prayojana* (ultimate objective), which is *prema*. Therefore only Kṛṣṇa is *para-tattva*, and all others are His parts, plenary portions, or shadow potencies such as Brahmā.

There is also *sādhya-bhrama*, which is illusion in regards to how one will attain his ultimate goal. How will one meet Kṛṣṇa? Not by giving charity, not by performing pious activity, not by travelling to holy places, not by studying scriptures or by any other method. The only way in Kali-yuga is performance of *harināma-saṅkīrtana*. Our basic foodstuff may be *roṭi*, but with that there should be some dahl, some *sabjī* and also some milk. These other preparations are necessary to make the meal complete. Therefore the instruction "Only chant *harināma*!" is given, but understand that included within the chanting of *harināma* are sixty-four kinds of *bhakti*. Within this *nāma* is everything; nothing remains outside of it. Taking shelter of the feet of a *guru*, the sixty-four kinds of *bhakti* and all of the thousands of devotional activities are included within it. Don't think that we will only take *harināma* and do nothing more. But we can condense those sixty-four kinds of *bhakti* into nine, and then again into five:

sādhu-saṅga, nāma-kīrtana, bhāgavata-śravaṇa
mathurā-vāsa, śrī-mūrtira śraddhāya sevana

sakala-sādhana-śrestha ei pañca aṅga
kṛṣṇa-prema janmāya ei pāñcera alpa saṅga

Śrī Caitanya-caritāmṛta (*Madhya-līlā* 22.128–9)

> One should keep the company of *sādhus*, chant *harināma*, hear *Śrīmad-Bhāgavatam*, reside in Mathurā and serve the deity of Bhagavān with faith. These five devotional activities are superior to the rest because even a slight performance of them awakens *kṛṣṇa-prema* inside one.

Of these, three are primary: *śravaṇam*, *kīrtanam* and *smaraṇam*. And then condensing it further, Rūpa Gosvāmī says that attaching the mind to the pastimes of Kṛṣṇa through *smaraṇam*, one should take *harināma*. And finally it is told that by taking *harināma* alone all perfection is attained. So within this one activity, there are many; a line is made of so many dots. Included within the performance of *nāma-saṅkīrtana* are the sixty-four varieties of *bhakti*, the path of *rāgānuga-bhakti*, and everything.

First of all there is *śravaṇam* – hearing from a *sad-guru* about these four kinds of *svarūpa-bhrama*: being illusioned concerning one's own inherent *svarūpa*, being illusioned concerning Bhagavān's *svarūpa*, being illusioned concerning the nature of one's *sādhana*, and not recognising things that are opposed to the healthy cultivation of *bhajana*. The knowledge of these four things constitutes the *tattva* of *śuddha-sādhana*. We must know what is opposed to *bhajana* or we will be lost, like the *sahajiyās* and so many others.

Next comes *asat-tṛṣṇā*. *Tṛṣṇā* means hunger or thirst, and one should have hunger for keeping the company of *sādhus*, and for hearing, meditating on and singing the glories of Bhagavān.

prema-dhana vinā vyartha daridra jīvana

Śrī Caitanya-caritāmṛta (*Antya-līlā* 20.37)

Kṛṣṇa-prema is the only wealth; without it one's life is useless, and such a person can be said to be really living in poverty. "Prabhu, please accept me as Your servant and give me *prema* for You" – this is hunger in its pure form. In relation to food, there are some things that can be taken, such as certain tonics, which increase one's appetite, and there are other things, such as tea and coffee, which diminish one's hunger. Similarly, there are certain activities, such as hearing the glories of Bhagavān and taking His name, which increase one's hunger for *prema*, which is the real *tṛṣṇā*. But those things which diminish our hunger for *prema* are called *asat-tṛṣṇā*, and they are of four kinds:

aihikeṣv aiṣanā pāra-
trikeṣu caiṣaṇā 'śubhā
bhūti-vāñchā mumukṣā ca
hy asat-tṛṣṇāś catur-vidhāḥ

Śrī Bhajana-rahasya (2.9)

As long as these four remain, one will have no hunger for the *prema* of Bhagavān, and *bhakti* will not come in its pure form. Therefore we should make an effort to keep these four at a distance. The first is *aihika viṣaya*, which means worldly desires, and amongst them three are primary: *kanaka*, *kāmīni* and *pratiṣṭhā*. As long as the desire for these three exist within a devotee, *bhakti* will not manifest within him.

The next kind of *asat-tṛṣṇā* is called *pāratrika*, which means the desire for attaining heaven or liberation. We should keep the desire for these far away because they are detrimental for attaining *bhakti*. The next is *bhūti-vāñchā*, which means the desire for mystic perfections. We should simply offer our *praṇāma* to these perfections from a distance and put our full faith in the name of Bhagavān, which possesses all *śakti*. It possesses a *śakti* that cannot be found in anything else.

muktiḥ svayaṁ mukulitāñjaliḥ sevate 'smān
dharmārtha-kāma-gatayaḥ samaya-pratīkṣāḥ

Kṛṣṇa-karṇāmṛta (107)

Dharma, *artha*, *kāma*, *mokṣa* and the eight yogic perfections will remain standing behind a devotee saying, "Prabhu, when will I acquire the good opportunity to render service to you?" But we won't ever look in their direction. If we were to have access to these perfections in our present condition, we would certainly abandon our *bhakti*. Therefore, being kind, Bhagavān won't give us these perfections even though He has invested all of His *śakti* in His name. What will not come from chanting the holy name? If a sincere devotee requires some facility for his service, then Bhagavān will certainly supply it. He will definitely fulfil such desires for one who takes *harināma* purely. But for now Bhagavān sees that we still have so many *anarthas*, and therefore giving us any perfections would be detrimental to our *bhakti*. It is like a small child who desires to cut up some fruit to eat. Then his father takes the knife and begins to cut it for him, but the child insists, "No, no Father! I want to cut it myself!" But the father says, "My son, if I give you the knife you may harm yourself," and he continues to cut the fruit himself. We know that all *śakti* exists within the holy name, it is *cinmaya*; therefore, even though the fruit of taking the *nāma* may not be apparent to us now, we should know that there is a very great fruit coming from it. It is just that in our present condition we may not be fully experiencing it. Don't think that there is no *śakti* in *harināma*, or that there is no *śakti* in *hari-kathā*. It is there, but the *guru* and Bhagavān keep it a little hidden from us so that we don't make a mistake and harm ourselves.

There are two categories of liberation, and we should not desire either of them. The first is to think, "I am Brahman," and the second category includes *sārūpya*, *sārṣṭi*, *sāmīpya* and *sālokya*. We should keep the desire for all these at a distance as well. At first we are told that we should leave the desire for worldly pleasure and pursue the pleasure of *prema*, but really, we should abandon the desire for that pleasure also! When we have no desire whatsoever for our own happiness, then our service will go directly to Kṛṣṇa. We won't desire to reside in any realm other than Vraja, where Bhagavān is in His complete form. Everywhere else

He is in a partial form. All of this falls within *asat-tṛṣṇā*, and next we will explain *aparādha* and *hṛdaya-daurbalya*.

(2)

Having faith in *guru*, Vaiṣṇava, *harināma* and *śāstra* is the first part of the kingdom of *bhajana*. Included within the second part are taking initiation from a *guru*, serving him intimately and accepting instruction from him concerning our *sva-dharma* – "How should I perform *bhajana*? Who is our worshipful deity?" This second part of *sādhana-bhajana* is compared to the sunrise, which dissipates the darkness of ignorance. The darkness is caused by these four kinds of *anarthas*: *svarūpa-bhrama*, *asat-tṛṣṇā*, *aparādha* and *hṛdaya-daurbalya*.

Bhaktivinoda Ṭhākura describes four types of *aparādha*. The first is *nāma-aparādha*, and because most readers are probably already familiar with the ten kinds of *nāma-aparādha*, I won't explain them here. The second type of *aparādha* is the offence to the Vaiṣṇava, which is the most serious. Very few people would intentionally offend their *guru*, but in general people cannot recognise the greatness of a real *sādhu*. There are many saints in this world who are *niṣkiñcana* (possessionless), and who are completely free from pride and any desire for prestige, but to fully understand their greatness is very, very difficult. Generally people just detect some apparent faults in either their natures or appearances. But understanding the full glory of a real saint is very difficult even for the demigods, and unless one has himself become an elevated soul, he will not be able to understand. Sometimes it is even very difficult for elevated Vaiṣṇavas to understand. One must first be able to understand the gradation in Vaiṣṇavas, and upon recognising a real saint, be prepared to serve him. Otherwise one may consider a non-Vaiṣṇava to be a Vaiṣṇava, and a Vaiṣṇava to be a non-Vaiṣṇava.

The third type of offence is *aparādha* towards the *svarūpa* of Bhagavān. Because in our present condition we have no direct relationship with Bhagavān Himself, there is no possibility of committing offences to His *svarūpa*. But the *śrī vigraha* is also directly Kṛṣṇa, and this refers to offences committed in serving the deity. It is possible for a *kaniṣṭha-adhikārī* Vaiṣṇava to commit offences, but it is not possible for an *uttama-adhikārī* Vaiṣṇava to commit an offence. But who will pass judgement on what is an offence and what isn't? Once a saint fell asleep with his feet facing a mosque. Then a Muslim priest came and said, "Hey! You are sleeping with your feet pointing towards the mosque?"

The saint replied, "You please do one thing: place my feet so that they are pointing in a direction where there is no mosque and there is no Allah."

Becoming a little worried, the priest said, "But Allah and the mosque are only in that direction."

The saint replied, "My friend, is there any place where Allah is not?" That priest was bemused and just went away. For an ordinary man to have done this would have been an offence, but for such a *mahātmā* it was not. We should not impose our own ideas of what is correct and incorrect on them. The scriptures have benevolently given rules that are favourable to our spiritual welfare, but sometimes a devotee who has reached the stage of *bhāva* may transgress them. Quarrelling and fighting with Bhagavān is not proper, but sometimes it is seen that an elevated devotee may do this. Vaṁśī dāsa Bābājī Mahārāja and Gaura-kiśora dāsa Bābājī Mahārāja would quarrel with their own object of worship. Understanding this is very, very difficult. To do this would certainly be *aparādha* for those of us who are *kaniṣṭha-adhikārīs* and who have not yet passed through the darkness of ignorance.

The fourth kind of offence is *aparādha* towards other *jīvas* in general. Because Prahlāda Mahārāja was an *uttama mahā-bhāgavata* Vaiṣṇava, he could see the presence of his worshipful deity in the heart of every living entity, and in his worshipful deity he could see the presence of all living entities. This is the symptom of a *mahā-bhagavata*; it is a very elevated stage. We should never disturb another soul. If we do so for our own profit, then we will not be able to engage in *bhajana*. As *kaniṣṭha-adhikārīs* we should respect all *jīvas* as the residences of Bhagavān, so what to speak of the respect we will give to Bhagavān's devotees? So we should not commit any *aparādha* towards these four: Bhagavān Himself (meaning the *śrī vigraha*), the holy name, the Vaiṣṇavas and ordinary people. If one desires to be a Vaiṣṇava and to experience the sunrise in his *bhajana*, then all of these *anarthas* must be kept far away.

Next Śrīla Bhaktivinoda Ṭhākura describes *hṛdaya-daurbalya* (weakness of heart):

tucchāsaktiḥ kuṭīnātī
mātsaryaṁ sva-pratiṣṭhatā
hṛd-daurbalyaṁ budhaiḥ śaśvaj
jñeyaṁ kila catur-vidham

Śrī Bhajana-rahasya (2.11)

Those who are enlightened and elevated in *bhajana* have said that *hṛdaya-daurbalya* is of four kinds. The first is to leave Kṛṣṇa and *bhagavad-bhakti* and become attached to any worldly object, whether it be gross or subtle. Next is *kuṭīnātī*, which refers to the many different kinds of prohibited activities, such as keeping bad association. It can also mean dishonesty or cheating, and the desire for liberation is the primary form of this cheating.

The next kind of *hṛdaya-daurbalya* is *mātsarya*, which means seeing the good qualities in another and silently burning in envy. The last is *pratiṣṭhā*, the desire for prestige. Once all the demigods were welcoming Indra. Seating him on an opulent *siṁhāsana*, they offered him a garland composed of very large, fragrant flowers while repeatedly exclaiming, "Indra *kī jaya ho*!" Meanwhile Indra's *guru*, Bṛhaspati, approached and, seeing him coming, Indra began to think, "If he enters this assembly, then everyone will show respect to him and my prestige will be diminished." Understanding the feelings within his disciple, Bṛhaspati left there and vowed to never return. The demons came to know of this and said, "Today Indra has offended his own *guru*! Therefore we should attack immediately." So they attacked, and Indra fled away from heaven. But there was no place where he could go to escape the reaction to his offence. He had to take birth as a pig, and mate with female pigs. After suffering this reaction he was again brought back to heaven. Even Indra is affected by the desire for prestige, so what to speak of an ordinary man? One may be able to abandon everything else, but the desire for prestige may still remain. Therefore with great care we should endeavour to rid ourselves of this desire.

As one's *anarthas* gradually begin to disappear, exclusive sentiment for Kṛṣṇa will arise in the heart. Respect will be given to all, but only Kṛṣṇa will be our worshipful deity. But what else comes along with this? In the same way that we will be remembering Kṛṣṇa, we will also meditate on those who are near and dear to Him; we should have so much respect for them. Ultimately we should give even more importance to them than to Kṛṣṇa Himself, and then He will be so pleased with us. Otherwise *bhakti* will not come to us. There are many who claim to be followers of Kṛṣṇa, yet they don't respect His devotees such as the *gopīs*. But Bhaktivinoda Ṭhākura has gone as far as to say that those who worship Kṛṣṇa without Rādhā are mere atheists. They will never attain *bhakti*, not even ordinary *bhakti*. People who insist on worshipping Kṛṣṇa alone become irritated when they hear this, but this is what Bhaktivinoda Ṭhākura says. And if someone worships all the forms of Bhagavān along with Kṛṣṇa, then exclusive *bhakti* will never come to them either. Rūpa Gosvāmī has given the process for attaining exclusive *bhakti*:

tan-nāma-rūpa-caritādi-sukīrtanānu-
smṛtyoḥ krameṇa rasanā-manasī niyojya

Śrī Upadeśāmṛta (8)

One should engage the tongue in chanting *nāma-kīrtana* and the mind in deeply remembering the descriptions of Kṛṣṇa's pastimes. And together with this, one should have a strong feeling of one's own lowliness – "I am helpless; I am unable to meditate on Kṛṣṇa's pastimes. I am not capable of ridding myself of my *anarthas*, and lust, anger, greed, illusion and envy are swallowing me up. The desire for prestige is destroying me. O Gurudeva! O Vaiṣṇavas! O Gopīnātha! Hear my plea! Except for You there is no one who can save me!" First expressing these feelings sincerely, with tears in the eyes, is so necessary. Actually being able to meditate on Kṛṣṇa's pastimes comes later; in the stage of *bhāva* it starts to become possible. But without *śravaṇa*, *kīrtana* and *smaraṇa* of Bhagavān, a devotee will not be able to concentrate his mind in *sādhana*.

Sometimes we see that a devotee has some special *niṣṭhā* for one of the nine limbs of *bhakti*. He doesn't disrespect the other limbs, but has attained Bhagavān through exclusive practice of one of them. Prahlāda Mahārāja did so by *smaraṇa*, Śukadeva Gosvāmī by *kīrtana* and Parīkṣit Mahārāja by *śravaṇa*. But Bhaktivinoda Ṭhākura says that unless engaged in hearing, chanting *and* remembering, a neophyte devotee who aspires for the exclusive *prema* of Śrī Rādhā and Kṛṣṇa will simply not be able to absorb his mind in *bhajana*.

Service to the deity is of two types: *arcana-pūjana* and *bhāvamayī-sevā*. The Gosvāmīs did both kinds, but they taught that the glories of *bhāvamayī-sevā* are greater. Rūpa Gosvāmī installed the Govindajī deity, and Sanātana Gosvāmī installed Madana-mohana. In the morning they would offer *pūjā* to the deity in a regulated manner, and then after offering some prayers and *praṇāmas*, they would go out.

rādhā-kuṇḍa-taṭe kalinda-tanayā-tīre ca vaṁśīvaṭe
premonmāda-vaśād aśeṣa-daśayā grastau pramattau sadā
gāyantau ca kadā harer guṇa-varaṁ bhāvābhibhūtau mudā
vande rūpa-sanātanau raghu-yugau śrī-jīva-gopālakau

Śrī Ṣaḍ-gosvāmy-aṣṭaka (7)

Overwhelmed by the divine madness of *prema* and exhibiting symptoms of intense separation, the Six Gosvāmīs would constantly wander around Vraja singing the glories of Śrī Hari in great ecstasy. Sometimes they would be at the bank of Rādhā-kuṇḍa, sometimes at the shores of the Yamunā and sometimes at Vaṁśīvaṭa.

This is *bhāvamayī-sevā*. Raghunātha dāsa Gosvāmī served a *govardhana-śilā*, but by *bhāvamayī-sevā*. He saw Girirāja as Kṛṣṇa, and the *guñjā-mālā* as Rādhā. Giving the *guñjā-mālā* to Girirāja, what were his feelings? "Today I have arranged for Rādhā to meet with Kṛṣṇa." And how did They meet? Where is the *mālā* placed? At the chest of Kṛṣṇa, so he would feel, "Now Rādhā is at Kṛṣṇa's chest." With great ecstasy and crying, sometimes he would hold Girirāja up to his brow, and sometimes he would place Him on his head. Sometimes he would hold Girirāja close to his heart and bathe Him with his tears, and he was completely indifferent to everything of this world. This is *bhāvamayī-sevā*.

Bhaktivinoda Ṭhākura says that one should chant the *mahā-mantra* and all other *mantras* given to us by our *guru* – the *guru-gāyatrī*, the *gaura-gāyatrī*, the *gopāla-mantra* and the *kāma-gāyatrī* – with great love and adoration. They should be chanted with great feeling according to one's own particular *rasa*. Then the sun will begin to rise, meaning that by the influence of *sādhu-saṅga*, one's *ruci* has increased. He has renounced everything; he has abandoned his beloved wife and children, his affectionate mother and father, his home, his money, fine clothing and servants. But if he hasn't abandoned the cardinal *anartha* – *pratiṣṭhā* – he may again return to all of those attachments. But if he has no desire for *pratiṣṭhā*, yet still has some attachment for some other thing, then there is nothing to worry about. To enter the realm of *bhajana*, the desire for *pratiṣṭhā* must be abandoned. Śrīla Bhaktisiddhānta Sarasvatī Prabhupāda compared the desire for *pratiṣṭhā* to the stool of a pig. For a *sādhaka*, abandoning the desire for *pratiṣṭhā* is the most important thing. If he has done so, then soon the sun will be rising, meaning that soon *bhakti* will be arising within him. But if he has not rid himself of this desire, then he will remain in the darkness of night.

As one hears *hari-kathā* from scriptures like *Śrīmad-Bhāgavatam* and *Bhakti-rasāmṛta-sindhu* in the company of Vaiṣṇavas, then gradually his *anarthas* will disappear, *sambandha-jñāna* will arise within him and he himself will become an exclusive Vaiṣṇava. Then he will serve Kṛṣṇa by *bhāvamayī-sevā*, and he will begin to meditate on one particular form and pastime of Kṛṣṇa. In the *Dāmodarāṣṭaka*, Satyavrata Muni prays to Kṛṣṇa as He is being caught from behind by Yaśodā. Tying a rope around Kṛṣṇa's waist, she binds Him to the grinding mortar. He is crying, and when the *kājala* that decorates His eyes mixes with His tears, it is like the flowing currents of the Gaṅgā and Yamunā. Kṛṣṇa is taking long breaths, and due to this His earrings are swinging to and fro. His neck is decorated by three lines, and He is wearing a large flower-garland across His chest. Desiring to kiss the face of Kṛṣṇa as Yaśodā and the *gopīs* do, intense hankering arises in the heart of Satyavrata Muni. Offering *praṇāma* to Kṛṣṇa hundreds of times, he prays that realisation of the Bāla-gopāla form of Kṛṣṇa will always flow in his heart, and that Kṛṣṇa will grant *darśana* of that form to his eyes as well.

This type of meditation where one particular form and pastime of Bhagavān is concentrated on is called *mantramayī-upāsanā*. We can sing in glorification of only one pastime, but so many other pastimes spring from that one pastime, and the flow continues in all directions. In a continuous flow one pastime finishes and another begins. In the *bāla-līlā* of Kṛṣṇa, there are so many pastimes, and when one meditates in this way, realisation of all of those pastimes will come. This principle especially applies to *mādhurya-rasa*. Deeply remembering Kṛṣṇa's pastimes, the *gopīs* sat in meditation. In their meditation they passed through the stages of *āsana*, *prāṇāyāma*, *dhyāna*, *dhāraṇā*, *dhruvāsmṛti* and *samādhi*, and reached a stage of *samādhi* where one's eyes remain open. This kind of *samādhi* is possible while one is walking, sitting or whatever. They went to Kṛṣṇa in the night, and He said to them, "You are all supremely fortunate. You have come from afar, and you have not been hindered by any obstacle. You all came for My *darśana*, and you have received it. You have now seen the beauty of the forest at night. So many beautiful flowers are blooming, and all the birds are making the beautiful '*kala-rava*' sound. The waves of the Yamunā are gently flowing, and on them the lotuses are blooming. And do you know that I am Bhagavān? Have you heard it somewhere?"

"Yes, yes, we have heard it – from Garga Ṛṣi or Paurṇamāsī or someone – we have heard it, but we don't believe it. How is it possible for such a debauchee, thief and liar as You to be Bhagavān? We don't believe even one percent of it."

"So you have received My *darśana*, now please return to your homes. The supreme *dharma* for wives is to serve their husbands. It is a very dark night, and there are many dangerous creatures lurking."

rajany eṣā ghora-rūpā
ghora-sattva-niṣevitā

Śrīmad-Bhāgavatam (10.29.19)

Two meanings can be applied to what Kṛṣṇa says here. When the Sanskrit words are separated in a different way, *ghora*, meaning fearsome, becomes *aghora*, which means harmless. In the second meaning He is saying, "This forest is inhabited by harmless creatures such as peacocks and deer, and therefore you should stay." So He is simultaneously teasing and enchanting them with His clever words.

"You all return quickly! Otherwise your husbands will come searching for you. If they see you with Me, it will not be good for Me, and it will not be good for you either. Your *dharma* will be ruined, so quickly go!"

The *gopīs* replied, "If You are really Bhagavān, then with Your own mouth You have given this order:

sarva-dharmān parityajya
māṁ ekaṁ śaraṇaṁ vraja

Bhagavad-gītā (18.66)

Abandon all *dharma* and surrender exclusively to Me.

So then what error have we committed? In another place You have said that one should offer *pūjā* to the *guru* before offering *pūjā* to Bhagavān. We have never heard instructions as beautiful as those You have just given us; therefore we accept You as our *guru*, so we should stay with You and serve You first! Some say that You have spoken the words of the scriptures, and others say that the scriptures have emanated from Your breathing. We don't know which is true, but we have read in the scriptures that only Bhagavān is the husband of all husbands. So if You are really Bhagavān, then offering *pūjā* to You is our sole duty. We have also heard that those who serve Mukunda have no other debt upon them – no debt to the demigods, to their mother or father, or to anyone. If You do not accept our *pūjā*, then You will be disregarding what has been said in the scriptures. The reaction to this irreligiosity will come to You, and You will fall down from the path of *dharma*. We have left everything to be with You, and we have given three or four reasons why we are not at fault. So please tell us now what we should do."

The *gopīs* rendered Kṛṣṇa speechless, and then they began the *rāsa-līlā*. Then He vanished, and the *gopīs* began searching for Him. They began deeply remembering Him, like a *sādhaka* sitting in meditation. As they were remembering Him, they tasted *rasa* in their hearts and the ecstatic symptoms of *pulakita*, *romāñca*, *anubhāva* and all the *sattvika-* and *vyabhicāri-bhāvas* manifested. After some time Kṛṣṇa again appeared before them, and they asked Him, "Prabhu, some people are affectionate only to those who are affectionate to them, while others show affection even to those who are inimical to them. And then there are those who will not show affection to anyone. Which of these types are You?"

Kṛṣṇa said, "The first kind of friends who show affection to others only to benefit themselves are like merchants. They have no real love, no *dharma*, and share no real intimacy with others. When they perform *bhajana* for Bhagavān, they expect Bhagavān to quickly give them His direct *darśana*. And when He doesn't, they throw the deity of Bhagavān they were worshipping in the Yamunā. This is not love, and this is not *bhajana*. The second type, like parents and *gurus* who are naturally affectionate, are real friends, and one can have intimate relationships with them. And in the third category are four types: those who are *āptakāma*, those who are *ātmārāma*, those who are *guru-drohī* (inimical to their superiors) and those who are *akṛtajña* (ungrateful). Those who are *āptakāma* are *ṛṣis* who have no necessity to love or not love; they have no desires. Those who are *ātmārāma*, like the four Kumāras, are satisfied on the plane of *ātmā*. It has no meaning to them if others insult and abuse them, or if they are offered respect. Another is *guru-drohī*. Their parents and *gurus* have tried to give them everything, yet in return these people only become inimical to them. And finally, those who are ungrateful never honour the good that others may have done to them. My dear *sakhīs*, please understand! I am not even one amongst these six types."

The *gopīs* began laughing, and said, "No, You are not just one of these six types; we see that You are all six!"

Then Kṛṣṇa said, "O *gopīs*, you are the dearest to Me, and I am the dearest to you. For the purpose of increasing your *prema* for Me, I vanished from your sight, and from a hidden position I listened to you describe how much love you have for Me. It is like a poor man who suddenly becomes wealthy, and is very pleased. Then when someone takes his wealth away from him, he laments. In the same way, I only did this to increase your *prema* for Me. What to speak of one lifetime, in thousands of the demigods' lifetimes I will never be able to repay My debt to you. I am *bahu-niṣṭhā* (attached to many lovers), but you are all *eka-niṣṭhā* (attached to only one lover). I have so many devotees and dear ones from lower to upper whom I must see, but you have abandoned everyone for My sake. Besides Me you have no other, therefore in lifetime after lifetime I will never be able to repay you."

After this they again performed the *rāsa-līlā*, and Kṛṣṇa Himself served them for the entire length of one of Brahmā's nights. This type of meditation performed by the *gopīs* is called *svārasikī*. But first comes *mantramayī*, which means worshipping Kṛṣṇa by the *mantra* given by the *guru*. The higher type of meditation will come in the morning time of *sādhana*, when the darkness caused by one's *anarthas* has completely disappeared. To reach that stage one must practise numerous varieties of *sādhana* and constantly chant *nāma-saṅkīrtana*. Bhaktivinoda Ṭhākura says that one who desires to be an exclusive devotee must engage in *rāgānuga-bhajana*. Without *rāgānugā*, the sentiment of exclusiveness will not come and one's *bhajana* will be included within *vaidhī-bhakti*. Then he will think, "Kṛṣṇa is Nārāyaṇa; there is no special difference between Them. He is also Rāmacandra and Nṛsiṁha." Beyond that he may think that there is no difference between Dvārakādhīśa and Govinda. As long as one hasn't come to know the special qualities of Govinda, then exclusive sentiment will not come to him.

Beyond this one may not be able to distinguish between Bāla-gopāla and Kiśora-gopāla. Those of us who desire to serve Śrī Rādhā and Kṛṣṇa will not serve a Bāla-gopāla deity, considering Him to be our son. Therefore we must understand what is exclusive sentiment, and to do that we must understand what is *rāgānugā*, and before that we must first understand what is *rāgātmikā*. *Rāgātmikā* devotees are those who reside in the spiritual world, and those who follow them while residing in this world are called *rāgānugā* devotees. Bhaktivinoda Ṭhākura says that *rāga* will arise through executing devotional activities. The meditation of a *rāgānugā* devotee is not opposed to the regulations of *vaidhī-bhakti*; it is only the feelings that are different. With *lobhamayī-bhakti* (devotion filled with spiritual "greed") a devotee will continue to perform all devotional activities and daily rituals. Mahāprabhu gave this instruction to Raghunātha dāsa Gosvāmī:

bāhya, antara, – ihāra dui ta' sādhana
'bāhye' sādhaka-dehe kare śravaṇa-kīrtana

'mane' nija-siddha-deha kariyā bhāvana
rātri-dine kare vraje kṛṣṇera sevana

Śrī Caitanya-caritāmṛta (Madhya-līlā 22.156–7)

Rāgānuga-bhakti is executed both externally and internally. Even though one may have attained perfection, externally he should still follow the regulations of *sādhana* such as hearing and chanting. But internally, in his perfected form, day and night he will be serving Kṛṣṇa in Vṛndāvana.

Bhaktivinoda Ṭhākura says that if one engages in *nāma-kīrtana* with great faith twenty-four hours a day, all of his *anarthas* will disappear. By the mercy of Kṛṣṇa, *bhāva* will arise inside him, and then performing *bhajana* will become very easy and natural. This is compared to the sunrise within a devotee's *sādhana*. At this point, Bhaktivinoda Ṭhākura moves a little upward in his description. In his *sādhana*, a *rāgānugā* devotee will deeply meditate on the morning pastimes of Kṛṣṇa and His associates. As he remembers these pastimes more and more, the sentiment of a particular *rāgātmikā* eternal associate such as Lalitā, Viśākhā, Nanda Bābā, Yaśodā, Subala, Śrīdāmā or Raktaka will begin to flow in his heart like an electric current. But at present that light is not lit in our hearts because the connection is not there. The bulb is in our hearts, and our *guru* is the one who makes the connection. The current comes through the medium of those devotees who practise *lobhamayī-bhakti*. When the *guru* presses the switch, at once the current of *bhāva* begins to flow.

It is early morning, and Śrīmatī is in deep sleep. Kṛṣṇa has returned to Nandagrāma after His evening pastimes and is also sleeping. Meanwhile, in the course of carrying out her morning duties, Rādhikā's maternal grandmother, Mukharā, approaches Her. She helped raise Rādhikā from infancy and also arranged Her marriage. Calling out, "My dear granddaughter, where are You?" she entered Rādhikā's home without any hesitation. There she saw Lalitā, Viśākhā, and numerous other *sakhīs* and *mañjarīs* sitting and waiting outside Rādhikā's room, meditating on their specific services to be performed when Rādhikā awakens. A *rāgānuga-sādhaka* will also sit in meditation like this in the morning while taking *harināma*. The *sakhīs* said to Mukharā, "Hey! Don't awaken Her! Be quiet!" But because Mukharā is older than them, she didn't listen and kept calling. Then Rādhikā slowly opened Her eyes; She was still very tired. Then Mukharā said, "Hey! What is this? Yesterday I saw Śyāma wearing this yellow shawl – how has it now come on the body of Rādhikā? Alas!" and she began to worry.

Then Viśākhā said, "O fool, you have really become old! Your vision is now distorted. The strong rays of the rising sun have come, and they have made Her cloth appear yellow." Then Viśākhā pointed at the sun, and while Mukharā turned her head to see, Viśākhā gave a signal with her eyes to Rūpa Mañjarī indicating, "Take away that cloth!" At once, within only one second, Rūpa Mañjarī removed the yellow cloth and replaced it with Rādhikā's usual blue shawl. Then Viśākhā said to Mukharā, "Just look! The light is better now – is Her cloth yellow or blue?"

Mukharā replied, "Yes – it really is blue." Being very embarrassed, she forgot why she had come to awaken Rādhikā in the first place and quickly departed. Then all of the *sakhīs* began laughing, "Just see how our *priyā* has belittled this old lady!" Then they said to Rādhikā, "Get up quickly! We must go now for our *sūrya-pūjā*. Quickly take Your bath; as soon as Your husband is finished milking the cows, he will be coming. We must clean the house." Rādhājī arose, and at once all of the *sakhīs* became present at Her side to render service. They placed a beautiful golden pot full of scented water from Mānasī-gaṅgā, Rādhā-kuṇḍa and the Yamunā there for Her to wash Her hands and face.

Then they saw that Śyāmalā, who is a *suhṛta* (friendly) *sakhī*, had come. Rādhikā stood up and embraced Śyāmalā, saying, "By meeting such a *sakhī* as you, this has become a very good morning indeed! And by your mercy it will become an even better morning. I planted a seedling of *prema*, and at once it grew into a big tree. It has very beautiful green leaves and flowers on its branches, but the fruit has not yet come; when will it bear fruit?"

Śyāmalā replied, "Oh, I think that You are not speaking truthfully! I see that this tree has very beautiful golden fruits, and that they are now ripe. I also see that You have been eating so much of this fruit that Your face has become discoloured. And it appears that the juice of this fruit has made Your eyes turn red (because You did not sleep last night). It also appears that this juice has been dripping on Your cloth, and that Your cloth has become dampened and stained. But You are trying to tell me that Your tree has not yet given any fruit?" In this way they discussed *rasa* between themselves.

Rādhājī said, "You are merely applying salt to My wounds. I am such a poor soul, and so unhappy. You are supposed to be helping Me, but you are just giving Me more misery. When the rainy season comes the clouds become very dark, and in the *amāvasyā* (new moon) night, there is no trace of the moon. When there is a flash of lightning, everything is illuminated, but afterwards it seems to be even darker than it was before. In the same way, I met Kṛṣṇa; but after meeting Him, what happened next, I simply don't know. When I came to My senses, I saw that I was sleeping in My home, and now I am more unhappy than I was before."

Śyāmalā said, "Oh, I understand. It is like when someone is so thirsty that they very quickly drink to their satisfaction, not paying any attention to the taste of the water, but simply drinking to quench their thirst. If anyone asks them, 'What did that water taste like?' they will reply that they did not notice. In the same way, You must have drank that *rasa* without tasting it, so again You will have to approach that *guru* Śyāma and this time pay attention to the taste. There is theoretical knowledge and practical knowledge. You are well-versed in theoretical knowledge, but You are not at all experienced, so You must approach Him again to learn."

Śrīmatī Rādhikā replied, "I am very weak-minded and I fear that black person. I don't want to accept Him as my *guru* and study from Him, but I see that you are so qualified, so mature and, unlike Me, you understand both theoretical and practical knowledge. So I think it would be better if you were to go and learn from Him and then return here to teach Me what you have learned."

Hearing all of this, the *sakhīs* and *mañjarīs* were tasting the same *rasa* that Rādhikā had tasted the night before, only they were drinking it through their ears. Then Śyāmalā embraced Śrīmatī Rādhikā and said, "*Sakhī*, I see that Your tree is full of fruit, and even if You are not seeing them now, within a few days You will certainly see that so many beautiful and sweet fruits have come." After saying this, Śyāmalā departed, laughing.

At that time Dhaniṣṭhā sent a *sakhī* to Śrīmatī Rādhikā to inform Her of Kṛṣṇa's position. That morning the news was that after Yaśodā kissed Kṛṣṇa's head, she said to Him, "O my dear child, the cows and your friends are waiting for You, but You are still sleeping!" Then she noticed some marks on Kṛṣṇa's mouth and thought, "These naughty boys must have scratched Him while wrestling, or perhaps while running after the cows He was scratched by thorns." At that moment Madhumaṅgala arrived calling, "O *sakhā*, O Kanhaiyā!" Seeing Mother Yaśodā pondering the scratches on Kṛṣṇa's mouth, Madhumaṅgala said, "I know where these marks have come from – He was playing with the *sakhīs*." In Sanskrit, the word *sakhi* can refer to both male and female friends, so Yaśodā thought that he was referring to Kṛṣṇa's cowherd boyfriends. Behind Yaśodā's back, Kṛṣṇa placed His forefinger to His lips, signalling Madhumaṅgala not to tell her, but Madhumaṅgala signalled back indicating, "I will disclose everything to her!" Kṛṣṇa was thinking that if Madhumaṅgala were to disclose the truth, it would be very shameful, so as Yaśodā went to fetch some water, He pulled Madhumaṅgala close and said, "If you don't disclose the truth, I will give you a *laḍḍu*, but if you do, I will certainly beat you!" and Madhumaṅgala laughed and kept the truth concealed. Then Kṛṣṇa took the water from Yaśodā, washed His mouth, drank something, ate some sweets which were prepared with butter, and went to Govardhana for the day.

As they were preparing Śrīmatī Rādhikā for Her daily duties, the *sakhīs* and *mañjarīs* were bathing in this *hari-kathā* being described by the *sakhī* sent by Dhaniṣṭhā. This is a summary of Śrī Rādhā-Kṛṣṇa's morning pastimes as described in *Govinda-līlāmṛta.* We will follow the path of *rāgānuga-sādhana*, not the path of *vaidhī-sādhana*, and eventually the sun of full realisation of these pastimes will arise in our hearts.

Chapter Eleven

The Final Day of Kārttika-vrata

Today is the day on which we complete our vow of *niyama-sevā* for the month of Kārttika. In the observance of this *niyama-sevā*, by the mercy of Bhagavān and especially by the mercy of *guru*, for the last month we have performed hearing and chanting of *hari-kathā* and taken *darśana* of all the primary places of Śrī Rādhā and Kṛṣṇa's pastimes in Vraja. Kārttika is the king of months, and its queen is Śrīmatī Rādhikā. This month is for the pleasure of Rādhikā, and whatever we have done for Her pleasure during the last month, we should continue doing for the remainder of the year. If in our hearts we consider ourselves very low and genuinely feel with great despair that "I have not yet attained Her mercy," then we have really been granted the fruit of following this vow.

Every day during this month we have sung the glories of Śrī Rādhā-Dāmodara in the form of the *Dāmodarāṣṭaka*, and tried to practise that *sādhana* which will awaken the desire in our hearts to always serve Śrīmatī Rādhikā. This is the final aim of all *sādhanas*. In the eleventh and final verse of *Śrī Upadeśāmṛta*, Śrīla Rūpa Gosvāmī describes the supreme spiritual desire, and how that desire can be fulfilled:

kṛṣṇasyoccaiḥ praṇaya-vasatiḥ preyasībhyo 'pi rādhā-
kuṇḍaṁ cāsyā munibhir abhitas tādṛg eva vyadhāyi
yat preṣṭhair apy alam asulabhaṁ kiṁ punar bhakti-bhājāṁ
tat premedaṁ sakṛd api saraḥ snātur āviṣkaroti

Śrī Upadeśāmṛta (11)

There are so many who are dear to Kṛṣṇa, but amongst them Rādhikā is the most dear to Him, and in the same way that Rādhikā is dear to Kṛṣṇa, Rādhā-kuṇḍa is also dear to Him. There is no special difference between Rādhā-kuṇḍa and Rādhikā Herself. Even though generally it is said that between Kṛṣṇa and *kṛṣṇa-nāma* there is no difference, there is really a small difference in mercifulness. The holy name is more merciful; Kṛṣṇa has invested all of His *śakti* in His *nāma*, and it is accessible to everyone at all times. By the mercy of the *nāma* we will attain the direct company of Kṛṣṇa, so therefore the holy name is more merciful. Similarly it is correct to say that Rādhikā and Rādhā-kuṇḍa are one and the same, but because this transcendental *kuṇḍa* appears in a physical form, it is more accessible to the conditioned *jīvas* of this world. Its water is accessible at all times and in all ways for our bathing, for our *ācamana* and for offering our prayers. Therefore the glories of Rādhā-kuṇḍa are even greater than those of Rādhikā Herself, and the *munis* have described it like this in the *Padma Purāṇa*:

yathā rādhā priyā viṣṇos
tasyāḥ kuṇḍaṁ priyaṁ tathā
sarva-gopīṣu saivaikā
viṣṇor atyanta-vallabhā

Amongst all the *gopīs*, Rādhikā is the best and most beloved of Kṛṣṇa. Therefore for someone to attain Her mercy is very rare; even for great souls such as Nārada it is rare. But if someone really desires that *prema*, that *rādhā-dāsya*, which even Nārada is praying for while performing austerities at Nārada-kuṇḍa, then if they bathe just once with great devotion in Rādhā-kuṇḍa, the *kuṇḍa* will bestow everything upon them. Is it not more difficult than that? After all, anyone can go there and bathe, but it must be ascertained whether or not we are really bathing with feelings of *bhakti*. If we bathe with great humility and faith, then those whose hearts are impure will become a little pure, those whose hearts are already a little pure will become a little more pure, and those whose hearts are completely pure will attain the direct service of Śrī Rādhā and Kṛṣṇa. The highest ideal was shown by Raghunātha dāsa Gosvāmī – how he left everything, took exclusive shelter of Rādhā-kuṇḍa, and said, "We desire nothing besides the mercy of Rādhikā":

tavaivāsmi tavaivāsmi
na jīvāmi tvayā vinā
iti vijñāya devi tvaṁ
naya māṁ caraṇāntikam

Śrī Vilāpa-kusumāñjali (96)

"O Srīmatī, I am Yours only, Yours only" – he wanted Rādhikā to hear him say this twice. "I cannot live without You, so please bring me to the shelter of Your feet and appoint me to Your service."

If we bathe at Rādhā-kuṇḍa, our hearts will become purified, an attraction for *rādhā-dāsya* will arise within us, and if we have similar feelings of pleading as Rūpa and Raghunātha dāsa Gosvāmīs had, then we will certainly attain Rādhikā's direct mercy. And this is especially true if it is done within this month of Kārttika.

Our goddess is Srīmatī; besides Her we have no other. In another place Raghunātha dāsa Gosvāmi prays:

he śrī-sarovara sadā tvayi sā mad-īśā
preṣṭhena sārdham iha khelati kāma-raṅgaiḥ
tvaṁ cet priyāt priyam atīva tayor itīmaṁ
hā darśayādya kṛpayā mama jīvitaṁ tam

Śrī Vilāpa-kusumāñjali (98)

O Śrī Rādhā-kuṇḍa, in a *kuñja* on your bank, immersed in great *prema* our worshipful goddess Śrīmatī Rādhikā sports with Her beloved Śrī Śyāmasundara. Since you are the dearest of all to Them, please mercifully grant me *darśana* of my mistress who is my very life and soul.

In one place, Rati Mañjarī, meaning Raghunātha dāsa Gosvāmī, has referred to Kṛṣṇa as Nātha, meaning "husband", but why is she addressing Him as Nātha? "You are the *nātha* of our worshipful goddess, Vṛndāvaneśvarī, and because we are related to Her, we are referring to You as Nātha also."

hā nātha gokula-sudhākara su-prasanna-
vaktrāravinda madhura-smita he kṛpārdra
yatra tvayā viharate praṇayaiḥ priyārāt
tatraiva mām api naya priya-sevanāya

Śrī Vilāpa-kusumāñjali (100)

O Nātha! O nectar-moon of Gokula, whose cheerful lotus face smiles sweetly! O crown jewel of the merciful! If You are pleased with me, then give me this boon only: for the purpose of rendering service to my mistress, please take me to where You are lovingly sporting with Your beloved."

Here, taking the position of a *sādhaka*, he is praying to Kṛṣṇa in order to attain Rādhikā's service. All of the Gosvāmīs have prayed in a similar way, as did the son of Vallabhācārya, Viṭṭhalācārya:

śyāmasundara śikhaṇḍa-śekhara
smerahāsa muralī-manohara
rādhikā-rasika māṁ kṛpā-nidhe
sva-priyā-caraṇa-kiṅkarīṁ kuru

prāṇanātha-vṛṣabhānu-nandinī
śrī-mukhābja rasalola-ṣaṭpada
rādhikā-pada-tale kṛta-sthithiṁ
tvāṁ bhajāmi rasikendra-śekhara

Śrī Rādhā-prārthanā (2–3)

O Śyāmasundara! O You whose head is adorned with a peacock feather! Your face always holds a playful smile, Your flute-playing is enchanting and You are very expert in enjoying *rasa* with Śrīmatī Rādhikā. Because You are an ocean of mercy, please make me a *kiṅkarī* (maidservant) at the feet of Your beloved. You are the Lord of the life of the daughter of Vṛṣabhānu and are always greedy to taste the nectar of Her lips. O Rasika-śekhara, foremost of those who are *rasika*! I don't desire anything other than to always reside at the feet of Śrīmatī Rādhikā.

Rūpa Gosvāmī, Raghunātha dāsa Gosvāmī, Bhaktivinoda Ṭhākura and all of our *ācāryas* have prayed to Kṛṣṇa for this very thing, and have also prayed directly to Rādhikā Herself for it. In one place Raghunātha dāsa Gosvāmī says:

anārādhya rādhā-padāmbhoja reṇuṁ
anāśritya vṛndāṭavīṁ tat-padāṅkaṁ
asambhāṣya-tad-bhāva-gambhīra-cittān
kutaḥ śyāma-sindho rasasyāvagāhaḥ

If anyone desires to reside in Vṛndāvana, achieve the mercy of Rādhikā and be appointed to Her service, they must worship those places where the dust of Her feet is lying, such as the many beautiful *kuñjas* of Vṛndāvana where She has enjoyed pastimes with Śrī Kṛṣṇa. Bhaktivinoda Ṭhākura has written in his *Gītāvalī*:

rādhikā-caraṇa-padma, sakala śreyera sadma,
yatane ye nāhi ārādhilo
rādhā-padmāṅkita-dhāma, vṛndāvana yāra nāma,
tāhā ye nā āśraya karila (1)

Aspirants for *rādhā-dāsya* must take shelter of those places where Rādhikā has placed Her lotus feet, such as Rādhā-kuṇḍa, Śyāma-kuṇḍa, Yāvaṭa, Prema-sarovara, Saṅketa, Nandagrāma and Varṣāṇā. Rūpa and Sanātana Gosvāmīs would constantly wander around Vṛndāvana, and by staying in each place for only one day and night, the remembrance of different pastimes would always be arising within them.

rādhikā bhāva-gambhīra, citta yevā mahādhīra,
gaṇa-saṅga nā kaila jīvane
kemane se śyāmānanda, rasa-sindhu-snānānanda,
labhibe bujhaha eka-mane (2)

Those who have not taken shelter of the dust of Rādhikā's feet by worshipping these places, and who have not attained the association of a *rasika mahā-bhāgavata* Vaiṣṇava who is always immersed in the grave and deep *bhāva* of Rādhikā, will never become submerged in the ocean of *rasa*. Therefore we should pray to the *dhāma*, to Girirāja-Govardhana and the Yamunā, to the dust of Rādhikā's feet, to Viśākhā and Lalitā, to our *guru-paramparā*, to

Bhaktivinoda Ṭhākura and to our own *gurudeva* that we never desire anything besides *rādhā-dāsya.*

rādhikā ujjvala-rasera ācārya
rādhā-mādhava-śuddha-prema vicārya (3)

ye dharila rādhā-pada parama yatane
se paila kṛṣṇa-pada amūlya-ratane (4)

rādhā-pada vinā kabhu kṛṣṇa nāhi mile
rādhāra dāsīra kṛṣṇa, sarva-vede bale (5)

Those who very carefully worship Rādhikā's feet will meet Kṛṣṇa in the snap of a finger, but what does it mean to meet Kṛṣṇa? Where is Kṛṣṇa complete? Without Rādhikā is He complete? Therefore only where there is the *yugala-kiśora* (youthful couple) is Kṛṣṇa complete. Only by the mercy of Rādhikā will one be able to have Their *darśana* and attain the qualification to serve Them. Without the mercy of Rādhikā one will not be able to meet Kṛṣṇa – this is correct, but what do the Vedic scriptures declare? What to speak of just Rādhā, Her *dāsīs* can also be very instrumental in helping one to meet Kṛṣṇa. They will say, "Come – you can meet Him here. Stay just here – you won't meet Him anywhere else!" Sometimes Kṛṣṇa says to these *dāsīs*, "I belong solely to you. As you say, I will do." So what to speak of Kṛṣṇa's feelings towards Rādhikā Herself, who is the *ācārya* of *ujjvala-rasa.*

Sometimes when They play games like chess and tic-tac-toe together, Rādhikā says, "You don't know how to play, therefore I will not play anymore!" Sometimes Kṛṣṇa applies Her *tilaka*, and She says, "You haven't applied it correctly. It should be like this." In this way She instructs

Him, and is therefore the *ācārya* of *ujjvala-rasa*. Śrīmatī is the dearest to Kṛṣṇa, and without Her mercy one will not be able to successfully meet Kṛṣṇa. With this objective we worship Her during this month of Kārttika, aspiring solely for *rādhā-dāsya*.

Raghunātha dāsa Gosvāmī left his home and family at a very young age, and with great eagerness walked the entire distance from Kṛṣṇapura in Bengal to Jagannātha Purī to be with Caitanya Mahāprabhu. His parents had made so many plans to prevent him from going, but they could not stop him. His mother said, "He is married to a girl of heavenly beauty, and he has so much property and wealth. If these things don't keep him here, then he should be chained and watched over by a guard. Then he will never escape." But having more insight, his father said, "If being married to a girl of heavenly beauty cannot bind him, having opulence equal to that of Indra cannot bind him, our affection cannot bind him, and if he has really adopted the temperament of Mahāprabhu's followers, then how can mere chains bind him?"

Upon Raghunātha dāsa's arrival in Purī, Mahāprabhu placed him under the care of Svarūpa Dāmodara. Then, after witnessing more and more of Mahāprabhu's *līlā*, his tendency towards *rādhā-dāsya* became strengthened. Of course, we are looking at him from the angle of vision that he was a *sādhaka*, although he was an eternally perfected soul. Everything he did was exemplary for aspiring *sādhakas*. When after some time Mahāprabhu returned to Goloka, Raghunātha dāsa gave up eating. Then, in separation from Mahāprabhu, Svarūpa Dāmodara also left this world. Then

Raghunātha dāsa gave up even drinking water and sleeping, and soon he took shelter of Gadādhara Paṇḍita.

Day and night Gadādhara Paṇḍita was lamenting in separation from Mahāprabhu. Raghunātha dāsa would come and render service to him, and besides Gadādhara Paṇḍita there was no other shelter for him. But the fire of separation was burning very intensely in Gadādhara Paṇḍita's heart, and after a few days, calling out "Gaurāṅga! Gaurāṅga!", Gadādhara Paṇḍita also entered into the eternal *līlā*. Then Raghunātha dāsa felt, "Whatever strength I had has been taken away; now I will certainly die. I will give up my life by either jumping in the ocean or from a mountain-top." But then he thought again: "If I am to give up this life, why should I do it by jumping in the ocean? Instead I will go to Vṛndāvana where I will drown in the Yamunā. Or if I will give up my life by jumping from a mountain, it will not be from Caṭaka Mountain (in Purī). Instead I will go to Govardhana and jump from there."

When someone feels such intense separation from Bhagavān, then it can be said that they are really performing *bhajana*. Whereas we, on the contrary, are mostly just eating, sleeping, joking and laughing all day long. We should make an effort to understand what the nature of these devotees' feelings of divine separation were. When a devotee is always thinking, "How will I meet Bhagavān?" with great eagerness, then it can be said that they are engaged in real *sādhana*. And we cannot even express the degree of Raghunātha dāsa Gosvāmī's *tṛnād api sunīcena*, his feelings of his own lowliness.

His heart burning in divine separation, he left Purī and walked all the way to Vṛndāvana, where he fell at the feet of Rūpa and Sanātana. Offering his very self to them, he said, "Now I cannot possibly be saved," but they showed him such affection that he was convinced not to give up his life. He began living with them, and just when the fire of his separation had cooled somewhat, Sanātana Goswāmī left this world. Again he was left feeling helpless. It seemed that whoever he tried to take shelter of would leave him, and he was feeling more separation than ever. Staying at Rādhā-kuṇḍa, day and night he was lamenting in separation, and then he heard that Rūpa Gosvāmī had also left this world. Now what remained for him? He wrote:

śūnyāyate mahā-goṣṭhaṁ
girīndro 'jagarāyate
vyāghra-tuṇḍāyate kuṇḍaṁ
jīvatu rahitasya me

Śrī Prārthanāśraya-caturdaśaka (11)

Now that I no longer have the sustainer of my life, the land of Vraja has become empty and desolate. Govardhana Hill appears like a great python, and Rādhā-kuṇḍa seems like the gaping mouth of a ferocious tigress.

Just see what his condition of divine separation was like! At that time he composed *Śrī Vilāpa-kusumāñjali*, and this verse appears near the end:

āśā-bharair amṛta-sindhu-mayaiḥ kathañcit
kālo mayāti-gamitaḥ kila sāmprataṁ hi
tvaṁ cet kṛpāṁ mayi vidhāsyasi naiva kiṁ me
prāṇair vrajena ca varoru bakāriṇāpi

Śrī Vilāpa-kusumāñjali (102)

"I had so many hopes, but one by one they have all vanished, and now everything is lost. All of the columns that I was grasping onto seem to have disappeared one by one, and now I am in a helpless condition. But if Śrī Rādhā and Kṛṣṇa would sprinkle just one drop of the ocean of Their *prema* on me, then all of my hopes would be completely fulfilled. What to speak of bathing in that fathomless ocean of nectar, if just one drop of it falls on my head or any of my limbs, then I will have attained that sustainer of my life which I have been longing for ever since I left my home and family. But then Mahāprabhu left me, Svarūpa Dāmodara left me, and when Gadādhara Paṇḍita also left me, I came here to Vṛndāvana where I took shelter of Sanātana Gosvāmī. But then he also left me, and now I am helpless. What was the nature of Sanātana Gosvāmī?

vairāgya-yug-bhakti-rasaṁ prayatnair
apāyayan mām anabhīpsum andham
kṛpāmbudhir yaḥ para-duḥkha-duḥkhī
sanātanas taṁ prabhum āśrayāmi

Śrī Vilāpa-kusumāñjali (6)

"I have never seen such an ocean of causeless mercy as Sanātana Gosvāmī. He showered all of his mercy upon me, and even though I had no desire to drink it, he made me drink the nectar of *bhakti* that Mahāprabhu came to give, which inspires one to fully renounce this world and which bestows spontaneous affection for the lotus feet of Śrī Rādhā and Kṛṣṇa. That inconceivably merciful Sanātana Gosvāmī who gave me a drink of the ocean of *bhakti-rasa* has left me, and now Rūpa Gosvāmī has also left me. Who can describe how merciful he was? He would always look after me with great care. Because I have taken *kṣetra-sannyāsa* here at Rādhā-kuṇḍa, he would regularly come here to give me his *darśana*. He was so merciful to me that he would show me his writings on the pretext of having me proofread them, and while reading them I would shed so many tears that the pages would become wet; but still I couldn't stop reading. Whatever I didn't receive directly from Mahāprabhu and Svarūpa Dāmodara, he bestowed upon me completely.

"Until now I have somehow sustained my life, but now that Rūpa Gosvāmī has left me, I can no longer remain in this world. This is my final condition. O Srīmatī! Now all I have left is You and Your *kuṇḍa*; otherwise I am completely helpless. For me to hold on to my life for even one more moment is very, very difficult. Somehow or other I have been sustaining it, but I can sustain it no longer. O Srīmatī! If You are not merciful to me at this very moment, I will give up this body at once! Why should I remain in Vṛndāvana? In the absence of Rūpa and Sanātana the *dhāma* appears like the gaping mouth of a ferocious tigress which is ready to devour me. And if You say that I should hold on to my life by reading prayers to Kṛṣṇa, I say what necessity do I have for Kṛṣṇa if I don't receive Your mercy? Therefore please be merciful to me at once."

This *Vilāpa-kusumāñjali* was his final prayer, and after completing it, he offered it to the lotus feet of Rādhikā. Generally poets reveal their last desires in their final compositions, and he desired nothing other than *rādhā-dāsya*.

Rūpa Gosvāmī also composed so many verses for Rādhikā, such as these:

rādhe jaya jaya mādhava-dayite
gokula-taruṇī-maṇḍala-mahite (1)
dāmodara-rati-vardhana-veśe
hari-niṣkuṭa-vṛndā-vipineśe (2)

Rādhā's appearance is so attractive from head to toe that upon seeing Her, Kṛṣṇa is immersed in *prema.* She is the increaser of *rati* in Dāmodara. The highest result of all types of worship is *rati* for the lotus feet of Kṛṣṇa, and the bestower of that *rati* is Rādhikā. In reality Kṛṣṇa is *āptakāma*, meaning that He has no unfulfilled desire, but upon seeing Rādhikā, not only one desire, but millions and millions of desires arise in Him. His quality of being *āptakāma* is demolished and He is drowned in the waves of desire.

vṛṣabhānūdadhi-nava-śaśi-lekhe
lalitā-sakhi guṇa-ramita-viśākhe (3)

Rādhikā arose like a new moon from the ocean of Vṛṣabhānu Mahārāja, and is so wonderfully attractive that it seems She showers nectar in all directions. Why is the name of Vṛṣabhānu mentioned in this verse? The *vātsalya-bhāva* of Yaśodā is stronger than that of Nanda Bābā. From the time Kṛṣṇa took birth, Yaśodā raised Him and He was the cynosure of her eyes. Therefore there is more *bhāva* and sweetness in the name Yaśodā-nandana than there is in the name Nanda-nandana, and even Nanda Bābā himself accepted that Yaśodā's love for Kṛṣṇa was greater than his. Sometimes Yaśodā would scold Kṛṣṇa and, taking very long breaths, He would begin crying. He would run to the lap of Nanda Bābā, who would ask, "My dear son, why are You crying? What happened? Did someone hit You?"

Whimpering, Kṛṣṇa would point in the direction of Yaśodā. "Your mother hit You? Then beware! Don't return to her! She beats You!" Then what would Kṛṣṇa do? With open arms He would run back to His mother and sit in her lap; that's how affectionate she was towards Him. She could bind Him with her love, but Nanda could not bind Him; He would only run back to His mother.

So in this song Rādhikā is referred to as Vṛṣabhānu-nandinī rather than Kīrtidā-nandinī for a similar reason. Because Vṛṣabhānu Mahārāja first found Her lying on a large lotus in the Yamunā, She always received more affection from him. First She would run to sit in his lap, and secondly to the lap of Kīrtidā. Śrīdāmā was Kīrtidā's dearest child, but Vṛṣabhānu Mahārāja always had more affection for Rādhikā.

Lalitā is a *parama-preṣṭha-sakhī*, and she even instructs Rādhikā. Without her mercy, it is not possible to attain *rādhā-dāsya*. To attain the position of serving Rādhikā, one must worship Lalitā, and if someone really desires to enter Vraja as a *dāsī* in the camp of Rādhikā, then Lalitā will be very merciful towards them. *Guṇa-ramita-viśākhe*: in calling out to Rādhikā, Rūpa Gosvāmī has also mentioned the name of Viśākhā because the same good qualities that exist in Rādhikā are also found in Viśākhā. They were born on the same day and are always together. She always serves Rādhikā with great *prema* and even instructs Her also. Without first approaching Viśākhā, one will not be able to attain the favour of Rādhikā Herself, so therefore her name has also been mentioned here.

karuṇāṁ kuru mayi karuṇā-bharite
sanaka-sanātana-varṇita-carite (4)

Rādhikā is the very embodiment of *karuṇā*, kindness, and every pore of Her every limb – indeed, every atom of Her existence – emanates *kṛṣṇa-prema*. But why have the names of Sanaka and Sanātana been mentioned? They are young *brahmacārīs*, appearing to be only five years old, and their hearts are very pure. They were exclusive devotees of Nārāyaṇa, but after they heard a description of Rādhikā's *aṣṭakālīya-līlā* from Śaṅkara, hankering for realisation of those pastimes arose within them. In the *Padma Purāṇa*, Śaṅkara described Her *aṣṭakālīya-līlā* to the Kumāras, and they in turn related it to Nārada Ṛṣi. They appeared long before Rūpa Gosvāmī, at the beginning of creation in Satya-yuga, and are well-known for being expert in describing Rādhikā's transcendental qualities. They narrated Her *aṣṭakālīya-līlā* – what could be greater than that?

Today we have made an effort to increase our "greed" for the service of Rādhikā, and when that hankering becomes complete, then our *darśana* of Vṛndāvana – including all of the places such as Sevā-kuñja and Girirāja-Govardhana that we visited this month – will have really become complete. We are actually unqualified in all ways for this, but if inside us a little of this hankering has arisen, then today we will say a special prayer to Lalitā, Viśākhā, all of the *gurus* in our *paramparā*, and especially to our own *guru-pādapadma*, that by their mercy this hankering will become complete. With this very hope we will not conclude our *vrata* today, but instead we will commence it: "How will I attain the *dāsya* of Rādhikā? Wherever it is available, whether in heaven or in hell, I will certainly go there." Therefore today we pray to Śrī Śrī Rādhā-Vinoda-bihārī and all of Their devotees that our desire, the very aim of our *bhajana*, will be fulfilled.

GLOSSARY

A

ācārya – spiritual preceptor; one who teaches by example.

ānanda – spiritual bliss, ecstasy, joy or happiness.

anarthas – unwanted desires in the heart, which impede one's advancement in devotional life.

antaryāmī – the indwelling Lord, or Supersoul, who guides the activities of all living entities.

aparādha – (*apa* = against, taking away; *rādha* = flow of affection) an offence committed against the holy name, Vaiṣṇavas, the spiritual master, the scriptures, holy places or the deity.

aparādhī – one who commits *aparādha*, offences.

arcana – deity worship; one of the nine primary processes of devotional service.

ārati – the ceremony of offering a deity articles of worship, such as incense, lamp, flowers and fan, accompanied by bell-ringing and chanting.

āsakti – attachment; this especially refers to attachment to the Lord and His eternal associates.

āśrama – (1) the four stages of life within the Vedic social system; that is, *brahmacārī* (celibate student), *gṛhastha* (householder), *vanaprastha* (retired from household life) and *sannyāsī* (renunciant); (2) the residence of someone practising spiritual life.

āśraya-vigraha – the receptacle of love for Kṛṣṇa, the devotees.

aṣṭakālīya-līlā – the eternal pastimes that Kṛṣṇa performs with His associates in eight periods of the day.
ātmā – the soul.
avadhūta – an ascetic who often transgresses the rules governing ordinary social conduct.
avatāra – an incarnation; one who descends.

B

bābājī – a renunciant who lives a life of seclusion.
bāla-līlā – childhood pastimes.
bhagavad-bhajana – see ***bhajana***.
bhagavad-bhakti – see ***bhakti***.
bhagavan-nāma – the holy name of the Lord.
bhagavat-kathā – narrations describing the Supreme Lord.
bhajana – activity performed as loving worship of the Supreme Lord, especially the ninefold limbs of devotion headed by hearing and chanting.
bhakti – the performance of activities that are meant exclusively for the pleasure of the Supreme Lord Śrī Kṛṣṇa, which are done in a favourable spirit saturated with love and which are devoid of desire for fruitive gain or liberation.
bhakti-rasa – the mellows of devotion.
bhāva – (1) spiritual emotions, love or sentiments; (2) the intial stage of perfection in devotion (*bhāva-bhakti*).
brahma – the impersonal, all-pervading feature of the Lord, which is devoid of attributes and qualities. It is also known as Brahman.
brahmacārī – a member of the first *āśrama* (stage of life) in the *varṇāśrama* system; a celibate, unmarried student.

brāhmaṇa – the intellectual class amongst the four castes (*varṇas*) within the Vedic social system (*varṇāśrama*).
brahmāṇḍa – an egg-shaped material universe.

C

cādar – a shawl worn by men.
capātī – a thin cake of unleavened bread.
caturvedī-brāhmaṇa – a scholarly priest who is conversant with the four Vedas.
cinmaya – spiritual; transcendental.
cit-śakti – the potency that relates to the cognisant aspect of the Supreme Lord. By this potency, He knows Himself and causes others to know Him. Knowledge of the absolute reality is only possible with the help of this potency. Also known as *saṁvit-śakti.*

D

daṇḍa – a stick carried by *sannyāsīs*, renunciants in the fourth stage of life according to the Vedic social system.
daṇḍavat-praṇāma – prostrated obeisances.
darśana – seeing, meeting, visiting with, beholding.
dāsī – a female servant.
dāsya-rasa – love for the Lord that is expressed in the mood of a servant.
dhāma – a holy place of pilgrimage; the abode of Śrī Bhagavān where He appears and enacts His transcendental pastimes.
dharma – religion in general; the socio-religious duties prescribed in the scriptures for different classes of persons in the *varṇāśrama* system.

dhotī – a piece of cloth worn round the lower body, one end of which passes between the legs and is tucked in behind.
dīkṣā – receiving initiation from a spiritual master.
dīkṣā-guru – the initiating spiritual master.

G

gṛhastha – family life, the second stage of life in the Vedic social system.
gopas – the cowherd boys who serve Kṛṣṇa in the mood of intimate friends. This may also refer to the elderly *gopas* who serve Kṛṣṇa in the mood of parental affection.
gopī-bhāva – the mood of devotion for Śrī Kṛṣṇa possessed by the cowherd women of Vraja.
gopīs – the young cowherd maidens of Vraja headed by Śrīmatī Rādhikā, who serve Kṛṣṇa in the mood of amorous love. This may also refer to the elderly *gopīs* headed by mother Yaśodā, who serve Kṛṣṇa in the mood of parental affection.
gośālā – cowshed; a shelter for cows.
gosvāmī – one who is the master of his senses, a title for those in the renounced order of life. This often refers to the renowned followers of Caitanya Mahāprabhu who adopted the lifestyle of mendicants. Descendants of the relatives of such Gosvāmīs or of their hired servants often adopt this title inappropriately merely on the basis of birth. The leading temple administrators in India are thus popularly referred to as Gosvāmīs.
guñjā-mālā – a necklace of *guñjā*, which are small, bright-red seeds with a black patch on the top. *Guñjā* berries are

said to be representative of Śrīmatī Rādhikā.

guru-paramparā – the disciplic succession through which spiritual knowledge is transmitted by bona fide spiritual masters.

guru-pūjā – worship of the spiritual master.

guru-sevā – service rendered unto the spiritual master.

guru-tattva – the philosophical principles relating to the spiritual master.

H

hari-kathā – narrations of the holy names, form, qualities and pastimes of the Lord.

harināma – the holy name of the Lord, especially referring to the *mahā-mantra*.

J

jagad-guru – a spiritual master so qualified that he can act as *guru* for everyone in the world.

jīva – the eternal individual living entity, who in the conditioned state of material existence assumes a material body in any of the innumerable species of life.

jñāna – (1) knowledge in general; (2) knowledge leading to impersonal liberation.

K

kājala – lampblack applied as a cosmetic to the eyes.

kāma-gāyatrī – a confidential *mantra* received from the spiritual master at the time of second initiation.

kaniṣṭha-adhikārī – the neophyte practitioner of devotional life.

karatālas – hand cymbals used in congregational glorification of the Lord.

karma – (1) any activity performed in the course of material existence; (2) reward-seeking activities; pious activities leading to material gain in this world or in the heavenly planets after death; (3) fate; previous actions that yield inevitable reactions.

kathā – narrations of the activities of the Supreme Lord and His devotees.

kaupīnas – the loincloth of an ascetic.

kīrtana – congregational singing of the Lord's holy names, which is sometimes accompanied by music. This may also refer to loud individual chanting of the holy name as well as oral descriptions of the Lord's names, form, qualities, associates and pastimes. *Kīrtana* is one of the nine most important limbs of devotion.

kṛpā – mercy.

kṛṣṇa-tattva – the philosophy behind the nature of Śrī Kṛṣṇā.

kṣatriya – the second of the four *varṇas* (castes) in the *varṇāśrama* system; an administrator or warrior.

kṣetra-sannyāsa – the vow to remain in a single holy place for the duration of one's life.

kuṇḍa – a lake or pond.

kuñja – a grove or bower; a natural shady retreat, the sides and roof of which are formed mainly by trees and climbing plants.

kurtā – a collarless shirt.

L

laḍḍu – an Indian sweet made from chickpea flour.
laṅgoṭī – the loincloth of an ascetic.
lākha – one hundred thousand.
līlā – the divine and astonishing pastimes of Śrī Bhagavān and His eternal associates, which grant all auspiciousness for the living entity, which have no connection with this mundane world and which lie beyond the grasp of the material senses and mind.
lobhamayī-bhakti – devotional service imbued with intense desire or "greed".

M

mādhurya-rasa – the mellow of amorous love.
madhyama-adhikārī – the intermediate practitioner of devotional life.
mahā-bhagavata – the topmost devotee of the Lord.
mahābhāva – the highest stage of divine love.
mahājana – a great spiritual personality.
mahātmā – a great soul; a self-realised personality.
mandira – temple.
maṅgala-ārati – ceremonial worship of the Lord performed an hour or so before sunrise.
mañjarī – (1) a young maidservant of Śrīmatī Rādhikā; (2) a blossom.
mañjarī-bhāva – the mood of devotion possessed by the young maidservants of Vraja.
mantra – a spiritual sound vibration that delivers the mind from its material conditioning and illusion when repeated over and over; a Vedic hymn, prayer or chant.

maṭha – a monastery or temple.
māyā – the Lord's illusory potency, which influences the living entities to accept the false egoism of being independent enjoyers of this material world.
māyāvāda – the doctrine of impersonalism, also known as *advaitavāda.*
māyāvādī – one who advocates the doctrine of impersonalism.
mṛdaṅga – a clay drum used in congregational glorification of the Lord.

N

naiṣṭhika-brahmacārī – a lifelong celibate.
nāma-haṭṭa – a system of preaching where devotees hold public preaching programmes in their homes.
nāma-saṅkīrtana – the practice of chanting the holy name of Kṛṣṇa, especially congregational chanting.
niṣṭhā – firm faith; established devotional practice that does not waver at any time.
niyama-sevā – adhering to a particular set of devotional rules and regulations, usually referring to vows followed during the holy month of Kārttika.

P

paisā – a coin in Indian currency.
paṇḍita – a scholar.
pañcamī – the fifth day of a lunar half month.
parakīya-bhajana – worship performed in pursuance of the devotional moods of the cowherd women of Vraja, who have a paramour relationship with Śrī Kṛṣṇa.

parakīya-bhāva – paramour love; an amorous relationship outside of marriage.
parama-guru – the spiritual master of one's initiating spiritual master.
paramahaṁsa – a topmost, "swan-like" devotee of the Lord.
parikramā – circumambulation of holy places.
praṇāma – an obeisance.
prasāda – literally meaning mercy, especially refers to the remnants of food offered to the deity.
prema – divine love.
prema-bhakti – a stage of devotion that is characterised by the appearance of divine love (*prema*); the perfectional stage of devotion.
priya – dear friend.
pūjā – offering of worship.
pūjārī – a priest who formally offers *pūjā*, worship, to the deity form of the Lord.
pulakita, romāñca, anubhāva – symptoms such as horripilation experienced in an advanced state of devotional ecstasy.
pūrṇimā – the full moon day.
puspāñjali – an offering of flowers from cupped hands to the Lord or his exalted devotee.

R

rādhā-bhāva – the deep mood of Śrīmatī Rādhikā's devotion for Kṛṣṇa.
rādhā-dāsya – service rendered to Śrīmatī Rādhikā.
rāgānuga-bhakti – an elevated stage of devotion that is motivated by spontaneous attraction or love.

rāgātmikā – one in whose heart there naturally and eternally exists a deep spontaneous desire to love and serve Śrī Kṛṣṇa. This specifically refers to the eternal residents of Vraja.

rasa – the spiritual transformation of the heart that takes place when the perfectional state of love for Kṛṣṇa, known as *rati*, is converted into "liquid" emotions by combination with various types of transcendental ecstasies.

rasagullā – a ball of soft milk-cheese soaked in syrup.

rāsa-līlā – Śrī Kṛṣṇa's dance with the *vraja-gopīs*, which is a pure exchange of spiritual love between Kṛṣṇa and the *gopīs*, His most confidential servitors.

rasika – one who relishes the mellows of devotion (*rasa*) within his heart.

rati – (1) attachment, fondness; (2) a stage in the development of devotion that is synonymous with *bhāva*.

roṭi – Indian-style unleavened bread that is oven-baked.

ruci – taste; the fifth stage in the development of the creeper of devotion.

rūpānuga-bhakti – devotion that follows the particular devotional sentiment cherished within the heart of Śrī Rūpa Gosvāmī.

S

sabjī – cooked vegetables.

sac-cid-ānanda – that which is eternal, composed of spiritual consciousness and full of transcendental bliss.

sad-guru – a perfected spiritual master.

sādhaka – one who follows a spiritual discipline with the objective of achieving pure devotion for Śrī Kṛṣṇa.

sādhana – the practising stage of devotion, in which the various spiritual disciplines performed for the satisfaction of Śrī Kṛṣṇa are undertaken through the medium of the senses for the purpose of bringing about the manifestation of *bhāva*, spiritual love of God.

sādhu – a saintly person.

sādhu-saṅga – the association of holy personalities.

sādhya – the goal of one's spiritual practice.

sahajiyā – one who considers the stages of advanced devotion to be easily achieved and who thus sometimes imitates the external symptoms of spiritual ecstasy associated with those stages.

sakhā – a male friend, companion or attendant.

sakhī – a female friend, companion or attendant.

sakhya-rasa – love or attachment for Śrī Kṛṣṇa that is expressed in the mood of a friend.

śakti – potency.

sālokya, sāmīpya, sārūpya and ***sārṣṭi*** – the four types of liberation, respectively, of residing on the same planet as the Lord, becoming His personal associate, obtaining a spiritual form similar to His, and obtaining opulence similar to His.

samādhi – meditation or deep trance.

sambandha-jñāna – knowledge regarding the mutual relationship between the Lord, the living entities and the material energy.

sampradāya – a school of religious thought.

saṁskāra – impression on the mind of acts done in a former state of existence.

saṁvit- and ***hlādinī-śaktis*** – the Lord's cognisance and pleasure potencies, respectively.

sanātana-dharma – eternal religion, i.e. devotion unto Śrī Kṛṣṇa.

sandhinī – the potency by which the Lord maintains His own existence and the existence of others.

sannyāsa – renounced, ascetic life, the fourth stage of life within the Vedic social system.

śāstra – scripture, especially the Vedic sciptures.

sattva, rajas and ***tamasa*** – the three material modes of goodness, passion and ignorance, respectively.

sattvika- and ***vyabhicāri-bhāvas*** – external symptoms of the highest internal spiritual ecstasy.

sevā – service, attendance on, reverence, devotion to.

siddhānta – philosophical doctrine or precept; demonstrated conclusion; established end; admitted truth.

śikṣā-guru – instructing spiritual master.

siṁhāsana – throne.

śloka – a Sanskrit verse.

śraddhā – faith. This refers to faith in the statements of the scriptures that is awakened after accumulating pious merit through the performance of devotional activities over many births.

śrāddha – a ceremony in honour of and for the benefit of deceased relatives, in which the forefathers are offered *piṇḍa*, an oblation of rice or flour, which endows them with a body suitable to attain *pitṛ-loka*, the planet of the forefathers.

śravaṇam, kīrtanam and ***smaraṇam*** – the devotional limbs of hearing, chanting and remembering, respectively.

śrī vigraha – the deity form of the Lord.
śuddha-bhakti – pure devotion; that is, devotion which is unmixed with fruitive action or monistic knowledge and which is devoid of all desires other than the desire to provide Śrī Kṛṣṇa with pleasure.
śuddha-guru – a pure, authentic spiritual master.
śūdra – the working class, the last of the four occupational divisions within the Vedic social system.
sukṛti – devotional or pious merit.
sūrya-pūjā – worship of the sun god, Sūrya.
sva-dharma – one's intrinsic duty in life.
svakīyā-bhāva – the mood of devotion wherein the devotee considers the Lord to be her lawfully wedded husband.
svarūpa-siddhi – the advanced stage of devotional life in which a devotee's *svarūpa*, internal spiritual form and identity, becomes manifest.

T

tapasya – austerities.
tattva – truth, reality, philosophical principle; the essence or substance of anything.
tilaka – clay markings worn on the forehead and other parts of the body by Vaiṣṇavas, signifying their devotion to Śrī Kṛṣṇa or Viṣṇu, and consecrating the body as the Lord's temple.
trayodaśī – the thirteenth day of a lunar fortnight.
tulasī – a sacred plant whose leaves and blossoms are used by Vaiṣṇavas in the worship of Śrī Kṛṣṇa; the wood is also used for chanting beads and neck beads.

tulasī-mālā – chanting beads made of wood from the sacred *tulasī* plant.

U

uttama-adhikārī, uttama-bhāgavata – the topmost devotee, who has attained perfection in his devotion unto Lord Kṛṣṇa.

uttama-bhakti – the topmost devotion. This is described in *Bhakti-rasāmṛta-sindhu* (1.1.11) as follows: "The cultivation of activities that are meant exclusively for the pleasure of Śrī Kṛṣṇa, or in other words the uninterrupted flow of service to Śrī Kṛṣṇa, performed through all endeavours of the body, mind and speech, and through the expression of various spiritual sentiments (*bhāvas*), which is not covered by knowledge aimed at impersonal liberation (*jñāna*) and reward-seeking activity (*karma*), and which is devoid of all desires other than the aspiration to bring happiness to Śrī Kṛṣṇa, is called *uttama-bhakti*, pure devotional service."

V

vaidhī-bhakti – devotion that is prompted by the rules and prohibitions of scripture.

vaiṣṇava-dharma – the Vaiṣṇava religion, which has as its goal the attainment of love for Kṛṣṇa.

vaiśya – the third of the four *varṇas* (castes) in the *varṇāśrama* system; agriculturists or businessmen.

varṇāśrama – the Vedic social system, which organises society into four occupational divisions (*varṇas*) and four stages of life (*āśramas*).

vātsalya-rasa – feelings of parental love for the Lord.
vipralambha-bhāva – the loving mood that is felt when separated from one's beloved.
vipralambha-rasa – the mellow tasted when separated from one's beloved.
vraja-prema – the love of the residents of Vṛndāvana, particularly the love of the *gopīs*.
vrata – vow.

Y

yajña – a Vedic fire sacrifice.
yuga-dharma – the religious practice prescribed for a particular millennium. For instance, in the modern age of Kali, the *yuga-dharma* is the chanting of the Lord's holy names.

VERSE INDEX

I

J

K

L

M

N

P

R

S

T

V

Y

BOOK CATALOG 2003

Gauḍīya Vedānta Publications

Śrī Śrīmad Bhaktivedānta Nārāyaṇa Mahārāja

— and —

Śrī Śrīmad A.C. Bhaktivedānta Swami Prabhupāda

Books by Śrī Śrīmad Bhaktivedānta Nārāyaṇa Mahārāja

Jaiva-Dharma

The groundbreaking spiritual novel by Śrīla Bhaktivinoda Ṭhākura

Jaiva-dharma reveals the ultimate development of the path of pure devotion to the English-speaking world.

Hardbound, 5 x 7.5", 1077 pages, Bible paper, 8 color plates, glossaries of terms, indexes of quoted verses and general index. **$15.00**

Śrīmad Bhagavad-Gītā

With extensive commentaries

This edition of *Bhagavad-gītā* contains two commentaries: the *Sārārtha-varṣiṇī Ṭīkā* by Śrīla Viśvanātha Cakravartī Ṭhākura and the *Sārārtha-varṣiṇī Prakāśikā-vṛtti* by Śrīla Bhaktivedānta Nārāyaṇa Mahārāja.

Hardbound, 5.5 x 8.5", 1120 pages, 12 color plates. **$15.00**

Śrī Śrīmad Bhakti Prajñāna Keśava Gosvāmī

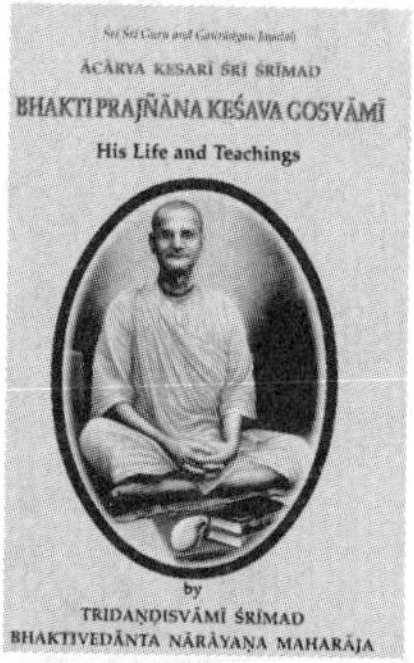

His Life and Teachings

A unique biography of a contemporary saint, the spiritual master of Śrīla Bhaktivedānta Nārāyaṇa Mahārāja and the *sannyāsa-guru* of Śrīla A.C. Bhaktivedānta Swami Prabhupāda.

Softbound, 5.5 x 8.5", 580 pages, 22 color illustrations. **$15.00**

Śrī Brahma-saṁhitā

Lord Brahmā's prayers of devotion to Kṛṣṇa

These prayers offered at the dawn of creation by Brahmā, the secondary creator of the universe, contain all the essential truths of Vaiṣṇava philosophy.

Softbound, 5.5 x 8.5", 452 pages. **$10.00**

Veṇu-Gīta

Tenth Canto, Chapter 21 of Śrīmad-Bhāgavatam

"By just hearing that flute-song that attracts the hearts of the whole universe, Sanaka and Sanandana and other *ātmārāma munis* became overwhelmed with joy and lost consciousness."

Softbound, 5.5 x 8.5", 188 pages, 8 color illustrations. **$10.00**

Bhakti-rasāmṛta-sindhu-bindu

A drop of the nectarean ocean of bhakti-rasa

This book is Viśvanātha Cakravartī Ṭhākura's summary of Śrīla Rūpa Gosvāmī's classic *Bhakti-rasāmṛta-sindhu* (*Nectar of Devotion*). Improved second edition.

Softbound, 6 x 9", 305 pages, 4 color plates, numerous diagrams. **$8.00**

Śrī Bhajana-rahasya

Deep analysis of the Hare Kṛṣṇa mahā-mantra

This revolutionary work by Śrīla Bhaktivinoda Ṭhākura presents an astounding analysis of the Hare Kṛṣṇa *mantra*, based on the eight verses of *Śrī Śikṣāṣṭakam*, covering all stages of *bhakti*.

Softbound, 5.5 x 8.5", 497 pages, 4 color plates. **$10.00**

The Origin of Ratha-yātrā

The world's most ancient religious festival

Lectures by Śrīla Bhaktivedānta Nārāyaṇa Mahārāja on the Ratha-yātrā, or the Cart Festival of Lord Jagannātha.

Softbound, 5.5 x 8.5", 372 pages, 8 color plates. **$10.00**

Śrī Prabandhāvalī

A collection of devotional essays

A translation of lectures spoken originally in Hindi, mostly on prominent dates from the Vaiṣṇava calendar. Improved second edition.

Softbound, 5.5 x 8.5", 203 pages, 4 color plates.
$6.00

Śrī Upadeśāmṛta

The ambrosial advice of Śrīla Rūpa Gosvāmī

Including the commentaries of Śrīla Bhaktivinoda Ṭhākura and Śrīla Bhaktisiddhānta Sarasvatī Ṭhākura, this book nicely complements Śrīla Prabhupāda's *The Nectar of Instruction*. Improved second edition.

Softbound, 5.5 x 8.5", 130 pages, 7 color plates.
$6.00

Bhakti-tattva-viveka

The true nature of devotion

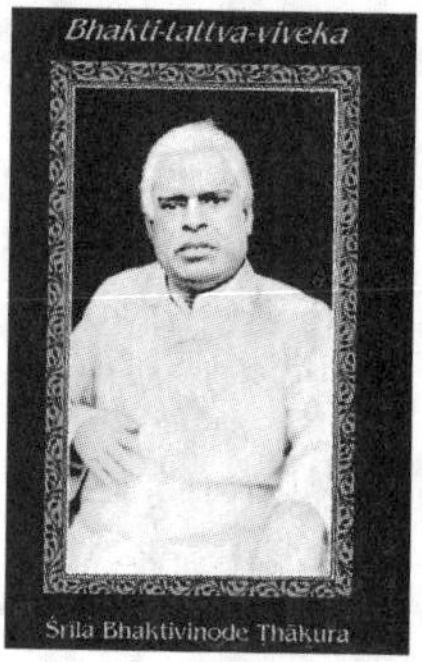

Śrīla Bhaktivinoda Ṭhākura has presented the grave and deep conclusions of devotional service, pure *bhakti*, in simple language that is accessible to any sincere reader.

Softbound, 5.5 x 8.5", 112 pages. **$4.00**

Śrī Manaḥ-śikṣā

Instructions to the mind by Śrīla Raghunātha dāsa Gosvāmī

Śrī Manaḥ-śikṣā consists of twelve verses composed by Raghunātha dāsa Gosvāmī that instruct the mind on how to make progress on the path of *bhajana*.

Softbound, 5.5 x 8.5", 153 pages. **$5.00**

Śrī Gauḍīya Gīti-guccha

An unprecedented collection of devotional songs

Sanskrit, Bengali and Hindi devotional poems, prayers, songs and *bhajanas* written by the Gauḍīya Vaiṣṇava *ācāryas* and compiled for the practicing devotee.

Spiral bound, 6 x 9", 224 pages. **$10.00**

Rays of Hope

A compilation of divine discourses, 1996–99

"The real connection with *guru* is through *bhāgavata-paramparā*. Even if one is not initiated by him in *guru-paramparā*, such a qualified disciple has understood his *guru's* mood."
– Śrīla Nārāyaṇa Mahārāja

Softbound, 5.5 x 8.5", 192 pages, 18 color photos and numerous illustrations. **$5.00**

Pinnacle of Devotion

An introduction to the most powerful yoga system

We all have a tendency to love, and no one can live without loving someone. The problem is, however, where to place our love.

Hardbound, 5.5 x 8.5", 200 pages. **$10.00**

Secret Truths of the Bhāgavatam

Discourses on Śrīmad-Bhāgavatam

A series of lectures by Śrīla Nārāyaṇa Mahārāja at the New Vraja community in Badger, California, in June 1999.

Softbound, 5.5 x 8.5", 192 pages, 16 color illustrations. **$5.00**

Jaiva-dharma, Part One

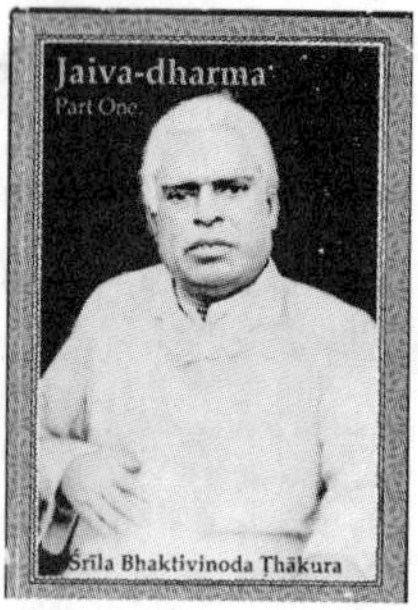

Part one of a spiritual novel by
Śrīla Bhaktivinoda Ṭhākura

"Out of all the books of Śrīla Ṭhākura Bhaktivinoda, *Jaiva-dharma* is considered to be the quintessence by religious thinkers of different countries."
– Śrīla Nārāyaṇa Mahārāja

Softbound, 5.5 x 8.5", 288 pages, 10 color illustrations. **$5.00**

Beyond Nirvāṇa

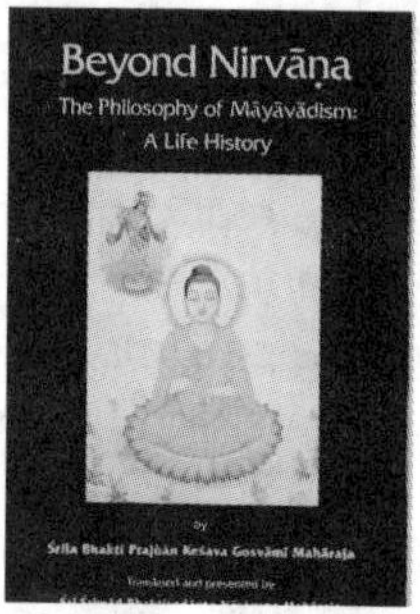

The new remake of Māyāvāda-jīvanī

Written by Śrīla Bhakti Prajñāna Keśava Mahārāja, this book soundly defeats impersonalist philosophy. Improved second edition.

Softbound, 6 x 9", 177 pages. **$10.00**

The Essence of All Advice

An historical collection of lectures

A series of lectures delivered in Badger, California based on Śrīla Prabhupāda's *The Nectar of Instruction.*

Softbound, 5.5 x 8.5", 250 pages. **$10.00**

My Śikṣā-guru & Priya-bandhu

Remembrances by Śrīla Bhaktivedānta Nārāyaṇa Mahārāja

A deep and revealing account of the intimate relationship between Śrīla Bhaktivedānta Nārāyaṇa Mahārāja and his instructing spiritual master and dear friend, Śrīla A.C. Bhaktivedānta Swami Prabhupāda, from 1947 up until final instructions given in 1977.

Softbound, 5.5 x 8.5", 49 pages. **$2.00**

Guru-Devatātmā

Accepting Śrī Guru as One's Life and Soul

Śrīla Bhaktivedānta Nārāyaṇa Mahārāja speaks on the importance of accepting a bona fide *guru*, who is more dear than life itself, the absolute necessity of second initiation, and other topics of *guru-tattva*.

Softbound, 5.5 x 8.5", 52 pages. **$2.00**

Our Gurus: One in Siddhānta, One in Heart

Clearing up the confusion

Nowadays some persons claim there are differences in the conclusions taught by Śrīla Bhaktivedānta Nārāyaṇa Mahārāja and Śrīla A.C. Bhaktivedānta Swami Prabhupāda. These authoritative responses to many of the objections will help the reader understand things as they are, without any politically motivated interpretation.

Softbound, 5.5 x 8.5", 61 pages. **$2.00**

Their Lasting Relation

An Historical Account

A detailed and nectarean account of Śrīla A.C. Bhaktivedānta Swami Prabhupāda's long-standing relationship with both his *sannyāsa-guru*, Śrīla Bhakti Prajñāna Keśava Gosvāmī, and Śrīla Bhaktivedānta Nārāyaṇa Mahārāja.

Softbound, 5.5 x 8.5", 49 pages. **$2.00**

Śrī Hari-Nāma Mahā-Mantra

The transcendental holy name of the Lord

"When a qualified person chants *harināma*, this light diffuses, thus keeping the darkness of illusion away from the soul."

Softbound, 5.5 x 8.5", 64 pages. **$2.00**

Happiness in a Fool's Paradise

The futility of material enjoyment

"Everyone wants to be happy, but generally we can find only a little happiness and affection in this world."

Softbound, 5.5 x 8.5", 32 pages, 6 color illustrations.
$2.00

To Be Controlled By Love

The guru–disciple relationship

"Even Kṛṣṇa, the Supreme Personality of Godhead, wants to be controlled by love and affection."
– Śrīla Nārāyaṇa Mahārāja

Softbound, 5.5 x 8.5", 32 pages. **$2.00**

The Butter Thief

The true nature of devotion

This book describes Kṛṣṇa's sweet childhood pastimes, in which He plays with Mother Yaśodā as an ordinary child.

Softbound, 5.5 x 8.5", 64 pages, 8 color illustrations.
$2.00

The Essence of Bhagavad-gītā

Absorbing the mind in Śrī Kṛṣṇa

"Absorb your mind and heart in Me, become My devotee, worship Me, offer your obeisances to Me, and certainly you will come to Me."

Softbound, 5.5 x 8.5", 32 pages, 4 color illustrations.
$2.00

Books by Śrīla A.C. Bhaktivedānta Swami Prabhupāda

These special editions are the authorized and approved versions, with the artwork and format specially designed by Śrīla Prabhupāda for introducing the Western world to Kṛṣṇa consciousness. Not one word or picture has been changed from Śrīla Prabhupāda's original version.

Kṛṣṇa: The Supreme Personality of Godhead

Who is Kṛṣṇa?

Śrīla Prabhupāda's summary of the entire Tenth Canto of *Śrīmad-Bhāgavatam*

Volume 1: hardbound, 7.5 x 10.5", 425 pages, 84 plates. **$15.00**

Volume 2: hardbound, 7.5 x 10.5", 400 pages, 24 plates. **$15.00**

Bhagavad-gītā As It Is

The most beloved of all Vedic literatures

Reprint of the historic original, authorized and approved 1972 Macmillan Complete Edition, with the original Sanskrit text, Roman transliteration, English synonyms, translation and elaborate purports.

Hardbound, 6.25 x 9.25", 1000 pages, 40 color illustrations. **$15.00**

Teachings of Lord Caitanya

The Golden Avatar

Lord Caitanya Mahāprabhu appeared in Bengal, India, in 1486, and began a revolution in spiritual consciousness that has profoundly affected the lives of millions.

Hardbound, 440 pages, many original color illustrations. **$15.00**

Kṛṣṇa, the Reservoir of Pleasure

Eternal enjoyment through transcendental sound

"Kṛṣṇa – this sound is transcendental. Kṛṣṇa means the highest pleasure. All of us, every living being, seeks pleasure. But we do not know how to seek pleasure perfectly." – Śrīla Prabhupāda

Softbound, 5.5 x 8.5", 32 pages. **$1.00**

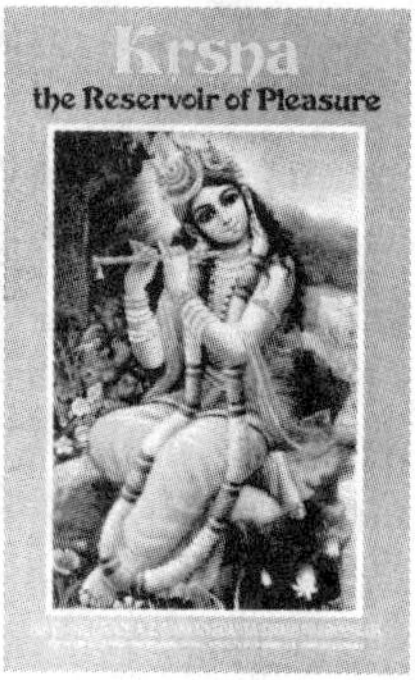

The Perfection of Yoga

"There have been many *yoga* systems popularized in the Western world, especially in this century, but none of them have actually taught the perfection of *yoga*." The original, authorized and approved version.

Softbound, 4 x 7", 56 pages, 8 color plates. **$2.00**

S. Regional Book Distributors

thwest (Seattle)
rk Hains
21 74th Ave. E
allup, WA 98373
n: Maitreya Muni Prabhu
ne: (866) HARIBOL (427-4265)
ail: maitreyamuni@yahoo.com

ifornia Northern (Berkeley)
stside & Company
9 Telegraph Ave. #D
keley, CA 94609
n: Kavidatta & Kṛtakarma Prabhus
ne: (510) 655-5018, 628-0671
ail: kavidatta2000@yahoo.com

ifornia Central (Badger)
Kailāsa Foundation
Box 99
ger, CA 93603
n: Nanda-gopāla Prabhu
ne: (559) 337-2448
ail: nandagopal@gaudiya.net

ifornia Southern (San Diego)
ayatra America
Box 2179
olla, CA 92038
n: Jayanta Prabhu
ne: (858) 518-5209
ail: jayantadasa@yahoo.com

ifornia Southern (Los Angeles)
VS
Dudley Ave
ice, CA 90291
n: Jaga-mohana Prabhu
ne: (310) 450-5371
ail: purebhakti@hotmail.com

th (Houston)
VS - Houston
19 Abergreen Trail
ston, TX 77095
n: Kṛṣṇa dāsa Prabhu
ne: (281) 550-2940
ail: kris4basics@hotmail.com

Eastern (Washington DC)
Rūpa-Raghunātha Gauḍīya Maṭha
6925 Willow St. NW
Washington, DC 20012
Attn: Vaṁśīvādana & Mukunda
Phone: (301) 864-3354
Email: ruparaghunatha@hotmail.com

South (Florida)
Acolapissa Foundation
PO Box 1689
Alachua, FL 32616-1689
Attn: Bhāgavata Prabhu
(386) 418-2046, (800) 814-7316 Ext. 00
Email: bhagavatdasa@msn.com

International Book Distributors

Canada - Western (Vancouver)
Stanley A. Gill
#25 - 15030 58th Ave.
Surrey, B.C. CANADA V3S 9G3
Attn: Prasasya Prabhu
Phone: (866) 575-9438
Email: stannshel@shaw.ca

Europe - UK (England)
Gour-Govinda Gauḍīya Maṭha
32 Handsworth Wood Rd.
Birmingham B20 2DS, UK
Attn: Jīva-pāvana Prabhu
Phone: (44) 121 682 9159
Email: gourgovinda@hotmail.com

Australia
Lee Handley
108 Byrill Creek Road
Uki, N.S.W. 2484 Australia
Attn: Līlāśuka Prabhu
Phone: (61) 266-797-025
Email: lilasuka@bigpond.com

International Spanish Distributors
Vedic Cultural Association
1002 S. Austin St.
Santa Ana, CA 92704 USA
Attn: Haridāsa Prabhu
Phone: (714) 775-8760
Email: hsalas1@prodigy.net

information on becoming a distributor in your area, email vd@regalgift.com or
1-800-681-3040, ext. 108.